EASY WAY TO CREATE AN EFFECTIVE PMO

PROJECT MANAGEMENT OFFICE

ANGELA SIRBU, MBA. PMP

© 2024 by Angela Sirbu, MBA. PMP. All rights reserved.

No part of this book may be reproduced or utilized in any form or by any means, electronic or mechanical, including photocopying, recording, or by any information storage and retrieval system, without permission in writing from the publisher.

First Edition 2024

Published by Angela Sirbu, MBA. PMP

CONTENTS

INTRODUCTION

CHAPTER 1: INTRODUCTION TO PMO

CHAPTER 2: PLANNING YOUR PMO

CHAPTER 3: PMO FRAMEWORK

CHAPTER 4: BUILDING THE PMO TEAM

CHAPTER 5: PMO PROCESSES AND METHODOLOGIES

CHAPTER 6: PROJECT SELECTION AND PRIORITIZATION

CHAPTER 7: IMPLEMENTING PMO TOOLS

CHAPTER 8: CHANGE MANAGEMENT IN PMO

CHAPTER 9: PMO GOVERNANCE

CHAPTER 10: PERFORMANCE MEASUREMENT AND REPORTING

CHAPTER 11: SCALING THE PMO

CHAPTER 12: RISK MANAGEMENT IN PMO

CHAPTER 13: PMO BEST PRACTICES

CHAPTER 14: CASE STUDIES AND REAL-WORLD EXAMPLES

CHAPTER 15: FUTURE OF PMO

INTRODUCTION

In the rapidly evolving landscape of modern business, the ability to manage projects efficiently and effectively has become a cornerstone of organizational success. Companies, both large and small, often grapple with the complexities of project management, seeking ways to streamline processes, enhance productivity, and achieve strategic goals. This is where the concept of a Project Management Office (PMO) becomes invaluable.

A well-structured PMO serves as the backbone of project management within an organization, offering a centralized framework that standardizes processes, improves resource allocation, and ensures that projects align with overarching business objectives. However, the establishment and maintenance of an effective PMO can seem daunting, especially for those who are new to the concept or have struggled with previous implementations.

"Easy way to create an effective PMO" is crafted with the intention of demystifying the process of setting up a PMO. This book is designed to be a practical guide, breaking down complex theories and methodologies into actionable steps that can be tailored to fit the unique needs of any organization. Whether you are a seasoned project manager, an executive looking to enhance your company's project capabilities, or a newcomer to the field, this book provides the insights and tools necessary to create a PMO that delivers tangible results.

Drawing on industry best practices, real-world examples, and expert advice, this book covers all facets of PMO creation and operation. From defining the strategic vision and securing executive buy-in, to developing processes, selecting the right tools, and managing change, each chapter is packed with valuable information. Additionally, it addresses common pitfalls and challenges, offering solutions to ensure your PMO not only gets off the ground but also thrives in the long term.

By the end of this book, readers will have a comprehensive understanding of what it takes to build an effective PMO, tailored to their organizational needs. They will be equipped with the knowledge to drive project success, foster collaboration, and ultimately, contribute to the sustained growth and competitiveness of their organization.

Chapter 1: Introduction to PMO

Definition and Purpose

A Project Management Office (PMO) serves as a centralized entity within an organization, designed to standardize project-related governance processes and facilitate the sharing of resources, methodologies, tools, and techniques. The essence of a PMO lies in its ability to provide structured support and oversight to ensure projects are executed efficiently, align with organizational goals, and deliver anticipated value. This subchapter delineates the definition and purpose of an effective PMO, underscoring its integral role in contemporary project management practices.

A PMO can be defined as a formalized body or department that is responsible for defining and maintaining project management standards across an organization. It functions as a repository of best practices, project status, and direction—ensuring that all projects align with the strategic objectives of the business. The establishment of a PMO is a strategic decision aimed at enhancing the overall project performance by implementing consistent project management practices and frameworks.

The purpose of a PMO extends beyond mere project oversight. It encompasses a broad spectrum of responsibilities, including strategic alignment, resource management, risk management, and performance measurement. One of the primary aims of a PMO is to ensure that projects are not only completed on time and within budget but also deliver the expected benefits and contribute to the strategic goals of the organization. This involves the meticulous planning and monitoring of projects, as well as providing the necessary support and guidance to project managers and teams.

A well-structured PMO provides a framework for project governance, which includes defining roles and responsibilities, establishing project management processes, and setting up performance metrics. This framework helps in maintaining consistency and quality across all projects, thereby reducing the likelihood of project failures. By implementing standardized processes, a PMO can streamline project execution, improve communication, and facilitate better decision-making.

Resource management is another critical function of a PMO. It ensures that project resources, including human, financial, and technical resources, are allocated efficiently and effectively. By maintaining a centralized resource pool, a PMO can optimize resource utilization, avoid conflicts, and ensure that the right resources are available for the right projects at the right time.

This not only enhances productivity but also contributes to the overall success of projects.

Risk management is an integral component of a PMO's responsibilities. It involves identifying potential risks, assessing their impact, and developing mitigation strategies to address them. A PMO provides a structured approach to risk management, ensuring that risks are proactively managed and that contingency plans are in place. This helps in minimizing disruptions and ensuring that projects stay on track despite uncertainties.

Performance measurement is essential for evaluating the success of projects and the effectiveness of the PMO itself. By establishing key performance indicators (KPIs) and metrics, a PMO can monitor project performance, identify areas for improvement, and make data-driven decisions. This continuous evaluation and feedback loop enable the PMO to adapt and evolve, ensuring that it remains relevant and effective in a dynamic business environment.

In essence, the definition and purpose of a PMO revolve around providing a structured approach to project management, ensuring strategic alignment, optimizing resource utilization, managing risks, and measuring performance. By fulfilling these roles, a PMO acts as a catalyst for achieving project success and driving organizational growth.

Types of PMOs

Project Management Offices (PMOs) serve as centralized units within organizations to standardize project management practices, facilitate project execution, and ensure alignment with strategic goals. The structure, function, and influence of PMOs can vary significantly depending on organizational needs, project complexity, and maturity levels. This subchapter delineates the primary types of PMOs, examining their distinctive characteristics, roles, and contributions to organizational project management.

Supportive PMO

Supportive PMOs, often referred to as consultative PMOs, provide a repository of best practices, templates, training, and lessons learned. These PMOs act as a knowledge hub, offering guidance and support to project managers and teams without exerting direct control over projects. They are typically found in organizations where projects are managed in a decentralized manner, and there is a need for consistency and standardization across projects. The supportive PMO's primary function is to enhance project management capabilities by offering expertise and resources, thus enabling project managers to execute their projects more efficiently.

Controlling PMO

Controlling PMOs exert a higher degree of influence over projects by enforcing compliance with organizational standards, methodologies, and governance frameworks. They implement project management processes, conduct regular audits, and ensure adherence to defined procedures. Controlling PMOs maintain a balance between support and control, providing both guidance and oversight to ensure that projects align with organizational objectives and regulatory requirements. These PMOs are suitable for organizations that require a consistent approach to project management and where adherence to standards is crucial for project success.

Directive PMO

Directive PMOs assume a more authoritative role by directly managing and executing projects. In this model, the PMO assigns project managers to projects, who report directly to the PMO rather than to functional departments. Directive PMOs are responsible for the overall success of projects, from initiation to closure, and have full control over project resources, schedules, and budgets. This type of PMO is prevalent in organizations where projects are highly complex, critical to business strategy, or require centralized control to ensure alignment with corporate goals. Directive PMOs often exist in industries with stringent regulatory requirements or where project failure can have significant repercussions.

Hybrid PMO

Hybrid PMOs combine elements of supportive, controlling, and directive PMOs to create a tailored approach that meets the unique needs of the organization. The hybrid model allows for flexibility in the level of control and support provided, depending on the project's nature, size, and strategic importance. This type of PMO can adapt to different project environments and maturity levels, offering a scalable solution that evolves with the organization's project management capabilities. Hybrid PMOs are particularly effective in dynamic environments where the ability to respond to changing demands and priorities is critical.

Enterprise PMO (EPMO)

An Enterprise PMO (EPMO) operates at the highest organizational level, overseeing the portfolio of projects and ensuring alignment with strategic objectives. The EPMO coordinates across multiple PMOs, departments, and business units to provide a cohesive approach to project management. Its responsibilities include strategic planning, portfolio management, resource allocation, and performance measurement. The EPMO ensures that projects contribute to the organization's long-term goals and maximizes the return on investment. Organizations with an EPMO benefit from a centralized view of all projects, enabling informed decision-making and prioritization of initiatives.

Understanding the different types of PMOs is crucial for organizations seeking to implement or optimize a PMO. Each type offers distinct advantages and can be aligned with specific organizational needs, project requirements, and strategic goals.

Benefits of a PMO

A Project Management Office (PMO) plays a pivotal role in enhancing organizational efficiency and effectiveness. One of the primary benefits of a PMO is the establishment of standardized project management practices. By implementing consistent methodologies, organizations can ensure that all projects are managed with a uniform approach, leading to more predictable outcomes and enhanced project success rates. Standardization also facilitates better communication and collaboration among project teams, as everyone adheres to the same set of guidelines and procedures.

Moreover, a PMO provides a centralized repository of project data and documentation. This centralization allows for more efficient tracking and reporting of project progress, enabling stakeholders to make informed decisions based on real-time information. The availability of comprehensive project data also aids in identifying trends, potential risks, and areas for improvement, thus fostering a culture of continuous improvement within the organization.

Resource management is another critical area where a PMO adds significant value. By overseeing the allocation and utilization of resources across multiple projects, a PMO ensures that resources are used optimally and that potential conflicts or bottlenecks are identified and addressed promptly. This holistic view of resource management helps in balancing workloads, preventing resource overallocation, and ensuring that critical projects receive the necessary attention and support.

Risk management is greatly enhanced through the establishment of a PMO. With standardized risk assessment and mitigation processes in place, organizations can proactively identify potential risks and implement strategies to mitigate them. This proactive approach to risk management reduces the likelihood of project delays and cost overruns, thereby safeguarding the organization's investments and enhancing project outcomes.

A PMO also contributes to improved stakeholder satisfaction by ensuring that projects are delivered on time, within scope, and on budget. By providing clear communication channels and regular status updates, a PMO helps to manage stakeholder expectations and address any concerns promptly. This transparency and accountability build trust and confidence among stakeholders, leading to stronger relationships and increased support for future projects.

Furthermore, the strategic alignment of projects with organizational goals is a key benefit of a PMO. By prioritizing projects based on their alignment with the organization's strategic objectives, a PMO ensures that resources and efforts are focused on initiatives that deliver the highest value. This alignment not only maximizes the return on investment but also enhances the organization's ability to achieve its long-term goals and objectives.

In addition to these operational benefits, a PMO fosters a culture of learning and development within the organization. By providing training, mentoring, and knowledge-sharing opportunities, a PMO helps to build the project management competencies of team members. This continuous professional development enhances the overall capability of the organization, making it more resilient and adaptable to changing market conditions and business needs.

The integration of technology and tools is another advantage offered by a PMO. By leveraging project management software and other digital tools, a PMO can streamline processes, automate routine tasks, and improve data accuracy. The use of technology also facilitates better communication and collaboration among geographically dispersed teams, enabling organizations to manage projects more effectively in a globalized business environment.

In essence, a PMO serves as a catalyst for organizational excellence by driving standardization, improving resource and risk management, enhancing stakeholder satisfaction, aligning projects with strategic goals, fostering a culture of continuous improvement, and leveraging technology. These benefits collectively contribute to the successful execution of projects and the achievement of organizational objectives.

Challenges in PMO Implementation

Establishing a Project Management Office (PMO) within an organization is often met with a myriad of challenges that can impede its efficacy and sustainability. These challenges can be broadly categorized into cultural, operational, and technical domains, each presenting unique obstacles that necessitate strategic resolution.

Cultural resistance is a significant barrier in PMO implementation. Organizational culture, deeply rooted in long-standing practices and attitudes, often exhibits inertia against new methodologies and structures. PMOs, by their nature, introduce standardized processes and oversight mechanisms that may be perceived as restrictive or intrusive by project teams and other stakeholders. Overcoming this resistance requires a nuanced approach that includes engaging leadership support, demonstrating the value of the PMO through quick wins, and fostering a culture of continuous improvement. Change management strategies, including effective communication and training programs, are crucial in aligning the organizational mindset with the objectives of the PMO.

Operational challenges are equally daunting. The integration of a PMO within existing organizational frameworks necessitates a thorough understanding of current processes and workflows. Misalignment between the PMO's objectives and the strategic goals of the organization can lead to inefficiencies and redundancies. Establishing clear governance structures, roles, and responsibilities is essential to mitigate these risks. Additionally, the PMO must be flexible enough to adapt to the evolving needs of the organization while maintaining its core functions. This balancing act requires robust planning, stakeholder engagement, and iterative refinement of PMO processes.

Resource allocation presents another operational challenge. PMOs often require significant investment in terms of personnel, technology, and training. Securing these resources can be difficult, particularly in organizations with constrained budgets or competing priorities. The PMO must demonstrate its value proposition to justify these investments. This can be achieved through metrics that highlight improved project delivery times, budget adherence, and overall project success rates. Furthermore, the PMO should advocate for a phased implementation approach, allowing for incremental resource allocation and the demonstration of progressive value.

Technical challenges in PMO implementation are primarily associated with the selection and integration of project management tools and technologies. The market offers a plethora of software solutions, each with varying capabilities and levels of complexity. Selecting the appropriate tool requires a comprehensive assessment of organizational needs, existing technological infrastructure, and user proficiency. Integration of these tools with existing systems, such as enterprise resource planning (ERP) and customer relationship management (CRM) systems, adds another layer of complexity. Ensuring seamless data flow and interoperability is critical for the PMO to function effectively. Adequate training and support mechanisms must also be established to facilitate the adoption of new technologies by project teams.

In addition to these challenges, PMOs must navigate the dynamic landscape of project management methodologies. The rise of agile frameworks, for instance, necessitates a shift from traditional waterfall approaches to more adaptive and iterative processes. This transition can be challenging for organizations with established project management practices. The PMO must facilitate this shift by providing the necessary training, tools, and support to project teams. Additionally, hybrid models that combine elements of both traditional and agile methodologies may be required to cater to diverse project requirements.

Addressing these challenges requires a holistic and adaptive approach. Continuous monitoring, feedback loops, and iterative improvements are essential to ensure the PMO remains aligned with organizational goals and capable of delivering sustained value. By effectively navigating cultural, operational, and technical challenges, organizations can establish a robust PMO that enhances project delivery and drives strategic success.

Case Studies

This subchapter delves into real-world applications of establishing an effective Project Management Office (PMO), illustrating the principles discussed in previous chapters through practical examples. The case studies selected represent diverse industries and organizational sizes, highlighting various challenges and solutions encountered during the PMO implementation process.

One notable example is from a mid-sized IT services company that struggled with project delays and budget overruns. The organization decided to establish a PMO to streamline processes and improve project outcomes. Initially, the PMO faced resistance from project managers who were skeptical about additional oversight. To address this, the PMO team focused on demonstrating value through small, quick wins. They standardized project documentation and introduced a centralized project tracking system, which led to significant improvements in transparency and accountability. Within six months, the company observed a 20% reduction in project delays and a 15% improvement in budget adherence.

Another case involves a large healthcare provider aiming to enhance its project portfolio management. The organization had multiple ongoing projects with overlapping objectives, leading to resource conflicts and inefficiencies. The PMO was tasked with optimizing resource allocation and aligning projects with strategic goals. By implementing a robust project portfolio management tool and establishing clear prioritization criteria, the PMO successfully reduced resource conflicts and improved project alignment with organizational objectives. As a result, the healthcare provider reported a 25% increase in project success rates and better alignment of projects with strategic initiatives.

A third example comes from a global manufacturing firm that sought to improve its new product development process. The company's projects often faced scope creep and quality issues, impacting time-to-market. The PMO introduced a stage-gate process to enhance project governance and control. This structured approach provided clear decision points and criteria for progressing through project phases. Additionally, the PMO implemented rigorous risk management practices and standardized quality assurance protocols. These measures led to a 30% reduction in time-to-market and a notable improvement in product quality, reinforcing the value of a disciplined project management approach.

The next case study focuses on a non-profit organization dedicated to environmental conservation. The organization had numerous projects funded by various donors, each with specific reporting requirements. The PMO was established to ensure compliance with donor requirements and improve overall project management practices. The PMO introduced standardized reporting templates and a centralized project management software to track progress and manage documentation. This initiative not only enhanced compliance with donor requirements but also improved project coordination and resource utilization. The non-profit reported a 40% increase in donor satisfaction and a significant improvement in project delivery timelines.

Lastly, a financial services company sought to enhance its regulatory compliance projects. The organization faced frequent regulatory changes, necessitating agile and responsive project management practices. The PMO adopted an agile project management framework to improve flexibility and responsiveness. They provided training for project managers and teams on agile methodologies and tools. This transition enabled the organization to respond more effectively to regulatory changes and deliver compliance projects on time. The financial services company reported a 35% reduction in project lead times and improved regulatory compliance.

These case studies underscore the critical role of a well-implemented PMO in driving project success across various contexts. By tailoring PMO practices to specific organizational needs and challenges, these examples demonstrate how effective PMO implementation can lead to significant improvements in project performance, resource utilization, and alignment with strategic objectives. Through careful planning, stakeholder engagement, and continuous improvement, organizations can harness the full potential of their PMOs to achieve sustained project success.

Chapter 2: Planning Your PMO

Assessing Organizational Needs

The establishment of an effective Project Management Office (PMO) necessitates a thorough understanding of organizational needs. A critical initial step involves a comprehensive assessment of these needs, which serves as the foundation for tailoring the PMO to align with the organization's strategic objectives and operational requirements.

To begin, it is essential to conduct an in-depth analysis of the current project management practices within the organization. This analysis should encompass a review of existing project management methodologies, tools, and processes. Key performance indicators (KPIs) and metrics should be evaluated to identify areas of strength and opportunities for improvement. This evaluation provides a baseline against which the effectiveness of the PMO can be measured post-implementation.

Stakeholder engagement is paramount during this assessment phase. Engaging with a broad spectrum of stakeholders, including senior management, project managers, team members, and clients, ensures a holistic understanding of the organizational landscape. Interviews, surveys, and workshops are effective methods to gather qualitative and quantitative data. The insights gained from these interactions help in identifying pain points, bottlenecks, and unmet needs within the current project management framework.

A gap analysis is a valuable tool in this context. By comparing the current state of project management practices with industry best practices and the organization's strategic goals, gaps can be identified. These gaps highlight specific areas where the PMO can add value, such as improving project delivery timelines, enhancing resource allocation, or increasing stakeholder satisfaction.

Assessing organizational maturity in project management is another critical aspect. Maturity models, such as the Capability Maturity Model Integration (CMMI) or the Project Management Maturity Model (PMMM), provide frameworks for evaluating the maturity level of an organization's project management processes. Understanding the maturity level helps in defining realistic and achievable objectives for the PMO, ensuring that it is neither under-ambitious nor over-ambitious.

The alignment of the PMO with the organizational strategy is crucial for its success. This alignment ensures that the PMO supports the overarching business goals and contributes to the strategic direction of the organization. A strategic alignment assessment involves mapping the organization's strategic objectives to the PMO's goals and functions. This mapping exercise helps in defining the scope and mandate of the PMO, ensuring that it is focused on delivering value in areas that are critical to the organization's success.

Additionally, it is important to assess the organizational culture and readiness for change. The PMO often introduces new processes, tools, and ways of working, which can be met with resistance if the organization is not prepared for change. Understanding the organizational culture and identifying potential barriers to change are essential for developing effective change management strategies. This includes communication plans, training programs, and support mechanisms to facilitate a smooth transition.

Resource assessment is also a key component of the needs assessment process. This involves evaluating the availability and capability of resources, including personnel, technology, and budget. Identifying resource constraints early on enables the organization to plan for necessary investments and allocate resources effectively.

In summary, assessing organizational needs is a multifaceted process that requires a systematic and comprehensive approach.

By conducting a thorough analysis of current practices, engaging stakeholders, performing gap and maturity assessments, aligning with strategic objectives, understanding organizational culture, and evaluating resources, organizations can lay a solid foundation for the successful establishment of an effective PMO. This foundational assessment ensures that the PMO is well-positioned to deliver value and drive project management excellence within the organization.

Setting Objectives

Establishing clear objectives is a critical component in the successful implementation and operation of a Project Management Office (PMO). Objectives serve as the foundation for all subsequent activities, guiding the PMO's direction and ensuring alignment with the broader organizational goals. The process of setting objectives for a PMO involves several key steps, each of which must be carefully considered to ensure the PMO's effectiveness and sustainability.

Initially, it is essential to conduct a thorough needs assessment. This involves gathering input from various stakeholders, including senior management, project managers, and other relevant personnel. The purpose of this assessment is to identify the specific challenges and opportunities that the PMO is expected to address. By understanding the pain points and strategic priorities of the organization, it becomes possible to formulate objectives that are both relevant and impactful.

Once the needs assessment is complete, the next step is to define the scope of the PMO. This involves determining the range of projects and activities that the PMO will oversee. A well-defined scope helps to prevent scope creep and ensures that the PMO remains focused on its core responsibilities. It is also important to consider the maturity level of the organization's project management practices, as this will influence the complexity and breadth of the PMO's objectives.

The articulation of specific, measurable, achievable, relevant, and time-bound (SMART) objectives is a best practice in this context. SMART objectives provide a clear and structured framework for evaluating the PMO's performance. For example, an objective might be to "reduce project delivery times by 15% within the next 12 months." Such an objective is specific, quantifiable, and time-bound, making it easier to track progress and assess outcomes.

In addition to setting SMART objectives, it is important to consider the alignment of PMO objectives with the strategic goals of the organization. This alignment ensures that the PMO contributes to the overall success of the organization and is perceived as a valuable asset by senior leadership. Objectives should be designed to support key business drivers, such as improving operational efficiency, enhancing customer satisfaction, or driving innovation.

Another critical aspect of setting objectives is stakeholder engagement. Objectives should be communicated clearly and consistently to all relevant stakeholders to ensure buy-in and support. This can be achieved through regular meetings, presentations, and documentation. Engaging stakeholders in the objective-setting process helps to build a sense of ownership and commitment, which is essential for the successful implementation of the PMO.

Furthermore, it is important to establish a mechanism for tracking and reporting on the achievement of objectives. This typically involves the development of key performance indicators (KPIs) and regular progress reviews. By monitoring progress against established objectives, the PMO can identify areas for improvement and make necessary adjustments to stay on track.

Finally, it is crucial to maintain flexibility in the objective-setting process. The business environment is dynamic, and organizational priorities may shift over time. Therefore, the PMO must be prepared to revisit and revise its objectives as needed to remain aligned with the evolving needs of the organization.

In summary, setting objectives for a PMO is a multifaceted process that requires careful planning, stakeholder engagement, and ongoing monitoring. By establishing clear, aligned, and measurable objectives, a PMO can effectively contribute to the strategic goals of the organization and drive project success.

Defining Scope

A precise definition of the scope is paramount to the establishment of an effective Project Management Office (PMO). The scope delineates the boundaries within which the PMO will operate, ensuring that its objectives are aligned with organizational goals and its resources are optimally utilized. The process of defining scope involves several essential steps, each contributing to a clear and comprehensive understanding of the PMO's responsibilities and limitations.

Initially, it is critical to engage key stakeholders in discussions to gather their expectations and requirements from the PMO. Stakeholders typically include senior management, project managers, and functional managers who have a vested interest in the successful implementation of the PMO. Through structured interviews, surveys, and workshops, stakeholders provide valuable insights into the challenges they face and the support they require from the PMO. This collaborative approach ensures that the scope is not only well-defined but also widely accepted across the organization.

Subsequently, the collected information must be meticulously analyzed to identify common themes and specific needs. This analysis aids in distinguishing between core functions and ancillary activities. Core functions generally encompass project governance, standardization of methodologies, performance monitoring, and resource management. Ancillary activities might include training, software tool implementation, and process improvement initiatives. Prioritizing these functions based on stakeholder input and organizational strategy is crucial for maintaining focus and avoiding scope creep.

Once the core and ancillary functions are identified, it is necessary to document the scope in a detailed and structured manner. A scope statement should be prepared, outlining the PMO's objectives, deliverables, and constraints. This document serves as a reference point for all future activities and decisions, ensuring that the PMO remains aligned with its defined purpose. The scope statement typically includes sections on the mission and vision of the PMO, the specific services it will provide, and the metrics for evaluating its success.

Defining scope also involves delineating the boundaries of authority and responsibility. The PMO must have a clear mandate regarding its decision-making powers and its role in relation to other departments and project teams. This clarity prevents overlaps and conflicts, fostering a cooperative environment. It is also essential to establish escalation procedures for resolving issues that fall outside the PMO's scope, ensuring swift and effective problem-solving.

Moreover, the scope definition process should incorporate a review of the existing project management landscape within the organization. Understanding current practices, capabilities, and pain points provides a baseline for the PMO's interventions. This review might reveal gaps in skills, tools, or processes that the PMO can address, thereby enhancing overall project performance.

Periodic review and revision of the scope are necessary to accommodate changing organizational needs and external conditions. As projects evolve and new challenges emerge, the PMO's scope must be flexible enough to adapt while remaining true to its core mission. Regular feedback from stakeholders and performance data should inform these revisions, ensuring that the PMO continues to deliver value.

Effective scope definition is a foundational step in creating a successful PMO. It requires thorough stakeholder engagement, careful analysis, clear documentation, and ongoing adaptability. By meticulously defining its scope, a PMO can position itself as a pivotal entity that drives project success and organizational excellence.

Resource Allocation

Resource allocation is a critical component in establishing an effective Project Management Office (PMO). It involves the strategic distribution of resources, including human capital, financial assets, and technological tools, to ensure the successful execution of projects. Proper allocation optimizes resource utilization, minimizes waste, and aligns with the organizational objectives, thereby enhancing the overall efficiency and effectiveness of the PMO.

A well-defined resource allocation strategy begins with a comprehensive assessment of available resources. This assessment should consider both current and projected resource availability, as well as the specific needs of ongoing and upcoming projects. Key factors to evaluate include skill sets, experience levels, budgetary constraints, and technological requirements. By understanding these variables, the PMO can make informed decisions about where and how to allocate resources to maximize productivity and project success.

One of the fundamental principles of resource allocation is prioritization. Projects should be ranked based on their strategic importance, potential impact, and alignment with organizational goals. High-priority projects should receive the necessary resources to ensure timely and successful completion, while lower-priority projects may be allocated resources on a more flexible basis. This prioritization process helps to focus efforts on initiatives that deliver the greatest value to the organization.

Effective communication is essential for successful resource allocation. Clear and transparent communication channels should be established between the PMO, project managers, and other stakeholders. Regular meetings and updates can help to identify any resource-related issues early on and allow for prompt adjustments. Additionally, fostering a culture of collaboration and openness encourages team members to share insights and suggestions, which can lead to more efficient resource utilization.

·

Another critical aspect of resource allocation is flexibility. The dynamic nature of projects often requires adjustments to resource distribution. The PMO should implement mechanisms for monitoring resource usage and project progress, enabling timely reallocation when necessary. Tools such as resource management software can provide real-time data and analytics, aiding in the identification of resource bottlenecks and facilitating swift corrective actions.

Risk management also plays a significant role in resource allocation. Identifying potential risks and their impact on resource availability allows the PMO to develop contingency plans. These plans should outline alternative resource allocation strategies to mitigate the effects of unforeseen events, ensuring that projects can continue without significant disruptions.

Training and development are vital for optimizing human resources. Investing in continuous education and skill enhancement helps to maintain a highly competent and adaptable workforce. The PMO should identify skill gaps and provide targeted training programs to address these deficiencies. This not only improves individual performance but also enhances the overall capability of the project teams.

Financial resource allocation requires meticulous planning and control. Budgeting should be based on realistic cost estimates and should include provisions for contingencies. The PMO must ensure that financial resources are allocated efficiently and that expenditures are tracked against the budget to prevent cost overruns. Regular financial reviews and audits can help to maintain fiscal discipline and accountability.

In conclusion, resource allocation is a multifaceted process that demands careful planning, prioritization, and flexibility. By implementing a structured approach to resource management, the PMO can enhance its ability to deliver projects successfully, thereby contributing to the organization's strategic objectives. Effective resource allocation not only optimizes the use of available assets but also fosters a culture of efficiency and continuous improvement within the PMO.

Timeline and Milestones

Establishing a Project Management Office (PMO) requires a systematic approach to ensure that all phases are executed efficiently and effectively. The timeline and milestones for creating an effective PMO are critical components that guide the organization through this complex transformation. This subchapter provides a detailed roadmap, highlighting key stages and their respective milestones.

The initial phase involves conducting a comprehensive needs assessment. This phase typically spans one to two months. During this period, the organization must identify its specific requirements for a PMO, align these needs with strategic objectives, and secure executive sponsorship. Key milestones in this phase include the completion of stakeholder interviews, the collection of baseline data on current project management practices, and the formulation of a preliminary PMO charter.

Following the needs assessment, the design phase commences. This phase can extend over two to three months. The primary objective here is to develop a detailed PMO framework tailored to the organization's needs. Milestones in this phase encompass defining the PMO's structure, delineating roles and responsibilities, and establishing governance policies. Additionally, the design phase involves selecting appropriate project management methodologies and tools, which are crucial for standardizing practices across the organization.

Once the design is finalized, the implementation phase begins. This phase is often the most time-consuming, lasting anywhere from three to six months. Key activities include the recruitment and training of PMO staff, the deployment of project management software, and the initiation of pilot projects to test the new framework. Milestones in this phase are marked by the successful onboarding of PMO personnel, the completion of training programs, and the full operationalization of PMO processes for pilot projects.

The next phase focuses on the integration of the PMO into the broader organizational environment. This phase typically lasts two to three months. The goal is to ensure that the PMO's processes and tools are seamlessly integrated with existing systems and that all departments are aligned with the new project management standards. Milestones include the integration of PMO tools with enterprise systems, the alignment of departmental processes with PMO standards, and the achievement of initial project successes under the new PMO framework.

The final phase is the optimization and continuous improvement phase, which is ongoing. The objective is to refine PMO processes based on feedback and performance data. Milestones in this phase are characterized by periodic reviews and audits, the implementation of process improvements, and the achievement of performance targets. Key activities include the establishment of a feedback loop for continuous improvement, regular performance reporting, and the adaptation of PMO practices to evolving organizational needs.

Throughout these phases, it is essential to maintain clear communication and regular updates to stakeholders. This ensures that all parties are informed of progress, challenges, and successes. Each milestone serves as a checkpoint to assess progress and make necessary adjustments, ensuring that the

PMO remains aligned with organizational goals and delivers the intended benefits.

By adhering to this structured timeline and focusing on key milestones, organizations can systematically build a robust and effective PMO that enhances project delivery capabilities and drives strategic success.

Chapter 3: PMO Framework

Governance Structure

The establishment of a Project Management Office (PMO) necessitates a robust governance structure to ensure effective oversight, strategic alignment, and accountability within the organization. A governance structure delineates the roles, responsibilities, and processes that guide the PMO's functioning, ensuring that it operates harmoniously with the broader organizational objectives. This subchapter delineates the foundational elements of an effective PMO governance structure, highlighting the key components and their interactions.

Central to the governance structure is the PMO Steering Committee, which serves as the highest decision-making body within the PMO framework. Typically comprised of senior executives and key stakeholders, the Steering Committee's primary function is to provide strategic direction and ensure that the PMO's activities align with the organization's strategic goals. The Committee is responsible for approving major projects, allocating resources, and resolving escalated issues that may arise during project execution. Regular meetings are convened to review the PMO's performance, address any systemic issues, and adapt strategies in response to changing organizational needs.

The PMO Director, reporting directly to the Steering Committee, plays a pivotal role in operationalizing the governance structure. The Director is tasked with the day-to-day management of the PMO, including the implementation of policies, procedures, and best practices. This role requires a comprehensive understanding of project management principles and the ability to coordinate across various departments and functions. The PMO Director ensures that project managers adhere to the established protocols and that project deliverables meet the predefined standards of quality, scope, and timeline.

Supporting the PMO Director are the Project Managers, who are responsible for the execution of individual projects. Project Managers ensure that their projects comply with the governance framework, including adherence to reporting requirements, risk management protocols, and performance metrics. They act as the liaison between the project team and the PMO, facilitating communication and ensuring that project objectives are met. The efficacy of Project Managers is critical to the overall success of the PMO, necessitating ongoing training and development to keep pace with evolving project management methodologies.

Integral to the governance structure is the establishment of standardized processes and procedures that guide project execution and monitoring. These processes include project initiation, planning, execution, monitoring, and closure. Standardization ensures consistency across projects, enabling the PMO to deliver predictable and repeatable outcomes. The governance framework also incorporates a robust risk management strategy, which involves the identification, assessment, and mitigation of potential risks that could impact project success. Regular risk assessments and contingency planning are essential components of this strategy.

Performance monitoring and reporting constitute another critical element of the governance structure. The PMO must establish key performance indicators (KPIs) and metrics to evaluate project performance and overall PMO effectiveness. Regular reporting mechanisms, such as dashboards and status reports, provide transparency and enable timely decision-making. These reports are reviewed by the PMO Director and the Steering Committee to ensure that projects are progressing as planned and to identify any areas that require intervention.

In summary, a well-defined governance structure is indispensable for the successful operation of a PMO. It provides the necessary framework for strategic alignment, resource allocation, risk management, and performance monitoring. By delineating clear roles, responsibilities, and processes, the governance structure ensures that the PMO can effectively contribute to the organization's strategic objectives and deliver value through successful project execution.

Roles and Responsibilities

In the establishment of an effective Project Management Office (PMO), delineating roles and responsibilities is paramount. A well-defined structure ensures clarity, accountability, and optimal performance across all project activities. This subchapter elucidates the primary roles within a PMO and their associated responsibilities, providing a blueprint for organizations aiming to enhance their project management capabilities.

The PMO Director is the cornerstone of the PMO. This role involves strategic oversight and alignment of the PMO's objectives with the organization's goals. The PMO Director is responsible for defining the PMO's vision, mission, and strategic direction. This includes setting performance metrics, ensuring resource allocation, and fostering a culture of continuous improvement. Additionally, the Director liaises with senior management and stakeholders to secure buy-in and support for project initiatives.

Project Managers within the PMO are tasked with the end-to-end management of projects. Their responsibilities encompass project planning, execution, monitoring, and closure. Project Managers develop detailed project plans, including scope, timelines, budgets, and resource requirements. They are accountable for risk management, ensuring that potential issues are identified and mitigated. Effective communication with stakeholders, team coordination, and adherence to project management methodologies are critical aspects of their role.

The role of the PMO Analyst is to provide analytical support and ensure data-driven decision-making within the PMO. PMO Analysts are responsible for collecting, analyzing, and reporting on project performance data. They develop and maintain dashboards and performance metrics, enabling real-time tracking of project progress. Their analysis helps identify trends, forecast outcomes, and recommend corrective actions. PMO Analysts also support project managers by providing insights into resource utilization, budget adherence, and risk assessment.

Resource Managers play a crucial role in optimizing the allocation and utilization of resources across projects. They are responsible for maintaining a comprehensive resource pool, including personnel, equipment, and technology. Resource Managers assess project requirements and allocate resources accordingly, ensuring that projects are adequately staffed and equipped. They also monitor resource utilization to identify bottlenecks and reallocate resources as needed to maintain project momentum.

The role of the PMO Coordinator involves administrative and logistical support to the PMO. PMO Coordinators manage documentation, scheduling, and communication within the PMO. They ensure that project documentation is accurate, up-to-date, and accessible to relevant stakeholders. Coordinators also facilitate meetings, prepare agendas, and record minutes. Their role is pivotal in maintaining organizational efficiency and ensuring that project activities are well-coordinated.

Stakeholder engagement is a critical function within the PMO, often managed by a dedicated Stakeholder Manager. This role involves identifying, analyzing, and managing stakeholder expectations and communications. The Stakeholder Manager develops engagement strategies, conducts stakeholder analysis, and ensures that stakeholder needs are addressed throughout the project lifecycle. Effective stakeholder management fosters collaboration, reduces resistance to change, and enhances project success.

Each role within the PMO contributes to a cohesive and efficient project management environment. Clear delineation of responsibilities ensures that all team members understand their contributions and can work synergistically towards common objectives. The establishment of these roles and responsibilities is a foundational step in creating a robust and effective PMO, capable of driving project success and organizational growth.

Processes and Procedures

A robust Project Management Office (PMO) hinges on the meticulous design and implementation of processes and procedures. These elements serve as the backbone, ensuring consistency, efficiency, and quality in project management practices across the organization. This subchapter delineates the essential processes and procedures that form the core of an effective PMO.

The initial step involves the establishment of standardized project management methodologies. These methodologies should align with industry best practices, such as those outlined by the Project Management Institute (PMI) or PRINCE2. Standardization facilitates uniformity in project execution, enabling project managers to follow a consistent approach, thereby reducing variability and enhancing predictability. The chosen methodology should be documented comprehensively, detailing every phase of the project lifecycle, including initiation, planning, execution, monitoring, and closing.

Next, the PMO must develop a suite of templates and tools tailored to support the standardized methodologies. These templates might include project charters, risk management plans, communication plans, and status reports. Tools such as Gantt charts, resource allocation matrices, and project dashboards should be made available to project teams. The objective is to provide a structured framework that simplifies project documentation, improves transparency, and streamlines data collection and reporting.

A critical component of PMO processes is the governance framework. This framework delineates the decision-making hierarchy, roles, and responsibilities within the PMO and across project teams. Clear governance structures ensure that accountability is established, and escalation paths are defined, thereby mitigating risks associated with ambiguity in leadership and oversight. Governance should also encompass performance metrics and Key Performance Indicators (KPIs) to monitor project progress and PMO effectiveness.

Resource management processes are integral to optimizing the utilization of human and material resources. The PMO should implement procedures for resource planning, allocation, and tracking. Resource management tools can aid in identifying skill gaps, forecasting resource demands, and balancing workloads across projects. By ensuring that resources are allocated efficiently, the PMO can minimize bottlenecks and enhance productivity.

Risk management is another vital process within the PMO framework. This involves the identification, assessment, and mitigation of risks throughout the project lifecycle. The PMO should establish a risk management plan that includes a risk register, risk assessment matrix, and mitigation strategies. Regular risk reviews and updates to the risk register help in proactively managing potential threats and ensuring that projects remain on track.

Communication procedures are essential for fostering collaboration and ensuring that stakeholders are informed and engaged. The PMO should define communication channels, frequencies, and protocols for both internal and external stakeholders. Effective communication plans promote transparency, facilitate information flow, and support decision-making processes. Regular status meetings, project updates, and stakeholder briefings should be integral components of the communication strategy.

Quality assurance processes are indispensable for maintaining high standards in project deliverables. The PMO should implement quality management plans that include quality control and quality assurance procedures. These plans should outline criteria for deliverable acceptance, testing methodologies, and review processes. By embedding quality checks at various stages of the project lifecycle, the PMO can ensure that outputs meet predefined standards and stakeholder expectations.

Continuous improvement processes should be embedded within the PMO to foster a culture of learning and adaptation. This involves regular reviews of PMO performance, feedback loops, and the incorporation of lessons learned into future projects. By systematically evaluating processes and outcomes, the PMO can identify areas for enhancement and implement changes that drive ongoing improvements in project management practices.

In sum, a PMO's effectiveness is significantly influenced by the rigor and comprehensiveness of its processes and procedures. Through the implementation of standardized methodologies, robust governance frameworks, efficient resource management, proactive risk management, clear communication protocols, stringent quality assurance, and continuous improvement mechanisms, the PMO can achieve its objective of driving project success and organizational excellence.

Tools and Technologies

The establishment of an effective Project Management Office (PMO) necessitates the utilization of specific tools and technologies that streamline processes, enhance collaboration, and ensure the efficient execution of projects. The selection of these tools should align with the strategic objectives of the PMO while also being adaptable to the dynamic nature of project management activities.

A robust PMO framework typically integrates project management software solutions that facilitate comprehensive planning, scheduling, and resource allocation. These platforms often include functionalities such as Gantt charts, Kanban boards, and time-tracking features, which provide project managers with the necessary oversight to monitor progress and address potential issues proactively. Widely adopted tools in this category include Microsoft Project, Jira, and Asana, each offering unique features tailored to varied project management methodologies.

Resource management tools are another critical component for an effective PMO. These tools assist in the optimal allocation of human and material resources, ensuring that projects are staffed adequately and resources are utilized efficiently. Tools like Smartsheet and Resource Guru provide capabilities for tracking resource availability, forecasting workload, and identifying potential bottlenecks, thereby enabling informed decision-making and strategic resource planning.

Collaboration and communication platforms are indispensable for fostering a cohesive project environment. Effective communication is paramount in a PMO setting, where multiple stakeholders and team members must remain aligned and informed. Tools such as Slack, Microsoft Teams, and Zoom facilitate real-time communication, file sharing, and virtual meetings, thereby enhancing collaboration and reducing the likelihood of miscommunication. These platforms also support integrations with other project management tools, creating a seamless workflow and ensuring that information is easily accessible.

Document management systems (DMS) are essential for maintaining project documentation, tracking changes, and ensuring regulatory compliance. Tools like SharePoint, Google Drive, and Dropbox offer secure storage solutions, version control, and collaborative editing features. These systems enable project teams to store, retrieve, and manage documents efficiently, thus ensuring that all project-related information is organized and accessible.

Risk management tools are vital for identifying, assessing, and mitigating potential risks that could impact project outcomes.

Software solutions such as RiskWatch and Active Risk Manager provide functionalities for risk identification, assessment, and monitoring, allowing project managers to develop proactive mitigation strategies. These tools often include risk registers, heat maps, and reporting capabilities, which aid in maintaining a comprehensive view of potential project risks.

Performance measurement and reporting tools are crucial for tracking project performance against predefined metrics and objectives. These tools enable PMOs to generate detailed reports, dashboards, and visualizations that provide insights into project status, budget adherence, and overall performance. Tools like Tableau, Power BI, and Crystal Reports offer advanced analytics and reporting features, empowering PMOs to make data-driven decisions and communicate project performance effectively to stakeholders.

The integration of these tools and technologies requires careful consideration of interoperability and user adoption. Ensuring that tools can seamlessly integrate with existing systems and workflows is essential for maximizing efficiency and minimizing disruptions. Additionally, providing adequate training and support to users is critical for fostering acceptance and proficiency in utilizing these tools.

By strategically selecting and implementing the appropriate tools and technologies, PMOs can enhance their operational effectiveness, improve project outcomes, and drive organizational success. The continuous evaluation and adaptation of these tools in response to evolving project management needs will ensure that the PMO remains agile and capable of meeting future challenges.

Performance Metrics

A successful Project Management Office (PMO) hinges on the establishment of robust performance metrics. These metrics serve as quantifiable measures that assess the efficiency, effectiveness, and overall success of the PMO in achieving its strategic objectives. The development and implementation of performance metrics involve a systematic approach that aligns with organizational goals, project outcomes, and stakeholder expectations.

Fundamentally, performance metrics for a PMO can be categorized into three primary domains: efficiency metrics, effectiveness metrics, and outcome metrics. Efficiency metrics focus on the operational aspects of project management, such as resource utilization, adherence to schedules, and cost management. Key indicators in this domain include the percentage of projects completed on time, budget variance, and resource allocation efficiency. These metrics provide insights into how well the PMO is managing its resources and adhering to project timelines.

Effectiveness metrics, on the other hand, assess the quality and impact of the PMO's processes and methodologies. This category includes metrics such as stakeholder satisfaction, process compliance, and the rate of project success. Stakeholder satisfaction can be measured through surveys and feedback mechanisms, while process compliance is evaluated through audits and reviews of project management practices. The project success rate is a critical indicator, reflecting the PMO's ability to deliver projects that meet predefined criteria of scope, quality, and stakeholder requirements.

Outcome metrics pertain to the broader impact of the PMO on organizational performance and strategic objectives. These metrics encompass the alignment of projects with strategic goals, the contribution of projects to organizational growth, and the return on investment (ROI) of the PMO. Metrics such as strategic alignment index, project portfolio performance, and ROI provide a macro-level view of the PMO's effectiveness in driving organizational success.

The selection of appropriate performance metrics necessitates a thorough understanding of the PMO's objectives and the specific needs of the organization. Metrics should be SMART (Specific, Measurable, Achievable, Relevant, and Time-bound) to ensure they provide meaningful and actionable insights. It is crucial to involve key stakeholders in the process of defining metrics to ensure alignment with organizational priorities and to foster a sense of ownership and commitment.

Data collection and analysis are integral to the effective utilization of performance metrics. The PMO must establish robust data collection mechanisms, leveraging project management software and tools to gather accurate and timely data. Regular analysis of this data enables the PMO to identify trends, pinpoint areas for improvement, and make informed decisions. Visualization tools such as dashboards and scorecards can aid in the clear and effective presentation of performance data to stakeholders.

Continuous improvement is a core principle in the management of performance metrics. The PMO should regularly review and refine its metrics to ensure they remain relevant and aligned with evolving organizational goals. Feedback loops, incorporating insights from stakeholders and project teams, are essential for the iterative enhancement of performance metrics.

In conclusion, the establishment and management of performance metrics are pivotal to the success of a PMO. By systematically defining, measuring, and analyzing these metrics, the PMO can ensure it operates efficiently, delivers effective project outcomes, and contributes significantly to the strategic objectives of the organization. Through a commitment to continuous improvement and stakeholder engagement, the PMO can maintain its relevance and effectiveness in a dynamic business environment.

Chapter 4: Building the PMO Team

Identifying Key Roles

In establishing a Project Management Office (PMO), a fundamental step involves the identification and delineation of key roles. This process is crucial to ensure the PMO operates efficiently and aligns with organizational goals. The roles within a PMO can be broadly categorized into strategic, managerial, and operational levels, each with distinct responsibilities and expectations.

At the strategic level, the PMO Director or PMO Executive is responsible for defining the overarching goals and vision of the PMO. This role involves aligning the PMO's objectives with the strategic direction of the organization. The PMO Director ensures that the PMO supports the organization's business strategy by prioritizing projects and allocating resources effectively. This position requires a deep understanding of both project management principles and the organization's strategic goals. The PMO Director is often involved in high-level decision-making processes and must possess strong leadership and communication skills to influence stakeholders and drive the PMO's vision forward.

The managerial level typically includes roles such as PMO Manager, Program Manager, and Portfolio Manager. The PMO Manager oversees the day-to-day operations of the PMO, ensuring that processes and procedures are followed, and that projects are executed efficiently. This role involves implementing project management methodologies, tools, and best practices across the organization. The PMO Manager also plays a key role in training and mentoring project managers and ensuring that they have the necessary skills and resources to succeed.

Program Managers are responsible for overseeing multiple related projects, ensuring that they are aligned and contributing to the overall program goals. This role requires a strong ability to manage complex interdependencies and coordinate efforts across different project teams. Program Managers must also monitor progress, manage risks, and ensure that program objectives are met on time and within budget.

Portfolio Managers, on the other hand, focus on the strategic alignment of projects and programs with the organization's goals. They are responsible for selecting and prioritizing projects within the portfolio to maximize value and ensure optimal resource utilization. Portfolio Managers must continuously assess the performance of projects and programs, making adjustments as necessary to align with changing organizational priorities.

At the operational level, the roles include Project Managers, Project Coordinators, and PMO Analysts. Project Managers are tasked with planning, executing, and closing individual projects. They are responsible for defining project scope, creating detailed project plans, managing project teams, and ensuring that project deliverables meet the required quality standards. Project Managers must also manage project risks, communicate with stakeholders, and ensure that projects are completed on time and within budget.

Project Coordinators support Project Managers by handling administrative tasks, such as scheduling meetings, maintaining project documentation, and tracking project progress. This role is essential for ensuring that Project Managers can focus on higher-level project management activities.

PMO Analysts provide analytical support to the PMO by collecting, analyzing, and reporting project data. They help in identifying trends, forecasting project outcomes, and providing insights that inform decision-making processes. PMO Analysts also play a crucial role in maintaining project management tools and systems, ensuring that accurate and up-to-date information is available to all stakeholders.

Clearly defining these key roles and their responsibilities is essential for the successful implementation and operation of a PMO. It ensures that all team members understand their roles and how they contribute to the PMO's objectives, ultimately leading to more effective project management and better alignment with organizational goals.

Recruitment Strategies

Effective recruitment strategies are fundamental to the successful establishment and operation of a Project Management Office (PMO). The recruitment process must be meticulously planned and executed to ensure the selection of individuals who not only possess the requisite technical skills but also align with the organizational culture and strategic objectives. This chapter delves into the various methodologies and best practices for recruiting PMO personnel, emphasizing the importance of a structured approach to talent acquisition.

A thorough understanding of the specific roles within the PMO is paramount. These roles typically include project managers, project coordinators, business analysts, and support staff. Each role requires a distinct set of skills and competencies. For instance, project managers must demonstrate strong leadership abilities, proficiency in project management methodologies such as Agile or Waterfall, and excellent communication skills.

Conversely, business analysts should possess analytical thinking, problem-solving capabilities, and a deep understanding of business processes.

To identify suitable candidates, a comprehensive job description must be crafted for each role. These descriptions should outline the primary responsibilities, required qualifications, and preferred experience levels. Additionally, they should reflect the organizational culture and values to attract candidates who are likely to integrate well with the existing team. Leveraging various recruitment channels, such as job boards, professional networks, and social media platforms, can broaden the candidate pool and increase the likelihood of finding the right fit.

The selection process should incorporate multiple stages to thoroughly assess candidates' capabilities and fit. Initial screening interviews can be conducted to evaluate basic qualifications and interest in the role. Subsequent stages should include in-depth technical interviews, behavioral interviews, and practical assessments. Technical interviews aim to gauge candidates' knowledge and problem-solving skills within the context of project management. Behavioral interviews focus on understanding candidates' past experiences, interpersonal skills, and cultural fit. Practical assessments, such as case studies or project simulations, provide insights into candidates' real-world application of their skills.

Involving key stakeholders in the recruitment process is crucial. Input from senior management, existing PMO staff, and cross-functional team members can provide diverse perspectives and ensure a holistic evaluation of candidates. This collaborative approach fosters a sense of ownership and alignment among team members, increasing the likelihood of successful integration of new hires.

Retention strategies should also be considered during the recruitment phase. Offering competitive compensation packages, opportunities for professional development, and a supportive work environment can attract high-caliber candidates and reduce turnover. Furthermore, clear career progression paths and regular performance feedback can motivate employees and foster long-term commitment to the organization.

Diversity and inclusion are critical components of an effective recruitment strategy. A diverse PMO team brings varied perspectives, enhances creativity, and improves problem-solving capabilities. Organizations should strive to eliminate biases in the recruitment process and actively seek to build a diverse workforce. Implementing structured interview processes, standardized evaluation criteria, and bias training for interviewers can aid in achieving this objective.

In summary, the recruitment of PMO personnel requires a strategic and methodical approach. By clearly defining roles, leveraging diverse recruitment channels, involving key stakeholders, and emphasizing retention and diversity, organizations can build a robust and effective PMO team. This foundational step is instrumental in driving the overall success and sustainability of the PMO, ultimately contributing to the achievement of organizational goals and objectives.

Training and Development

The establishment of a Project Management Office (PMO) necessitates a robust framework for training and development to ensure the effective execution of its functions. Training and development within a PMO context focus on equipping staff with the necessary skills and knowledge to manage and oversee projects effectively. This involves both initial training for new employees and ongoing development for existing staff to keep pace with evolving methodologies and technologies.

Training programs should commence with a comprehensive induction process that familiarizes new employees with the PMO's objectives, processes, tools, and the organizational culture. This foundational training should cover essential project management methodologies such as Agile, Waterfall, and Hybrid models, ensuring that staff can adapt to various project requirements. Additionally, training on specific project management tools, such as Microsoft Project, JIRA, or Asana, is crucial for efficient project tracking and management.

Ongoing development is equally critical and can be achieved through continuous professional development programs. These programs should include advanced training sessions, workshops, and seminars on emerging trends and technologies in project management. Participation in industry conferences and webinars can also provide valuable insights and networking opportunities, fostering a culture of continuous learning within the PMO.

Certifications play a significant role in the professional development of PMO staff. Encouraging and supporting employees to obtain certifications such as PMP (Project Management Professional), PRINCE2 (Projects IN Controlled Environments), or Certified ScrumMaster (CSM) can enhance their credibility and expertise. These certifications not only validate the staff's skills but also align the PMO's capabilities with industry standards.

Mentorship programs can further augment training and development efforts. Pairing less experienced staff with seasoned project managers allows for the transfer of tacit knowledge and practical insights that are not typically covered in formal training sessions. This mentor-mentee relationship can facilitate personal and professional growth, fostering a collaborative learning environment.

The use of case studies and real-world project simulations in training sessions can provide practical experience and reinforce theoretical knowledge. Analyzing successful and failed projects allows staff to understand the complexities of project management and learn from past mistakes and successes. Simulations, on the other hand, offer a risk-free environment to practice decision-making and problem-solving skills.

Performance assessments and feedback mechanisms are integral to the training and development process. Regular evaluations of staff performance can identify skill gaps and training needs, enabling the PMO to tailor its development programs accordingly. Constructive feedback helps employees understand their strengths and areas for improvement, promoting a culture of continuous enhancement.

E-learning platforms and online resources have become increasingly important in facilitating training and development. These platforms offer flexibility, allowing staff to learn at their own pace and convenience. Online courses, video tutorials, and interactive modules can cover a wide range of topics, from basic project management principles to advanced analytical techniques.

Incorporating a structured training and development strategy within the PMO not only enhances the competencies of individual staff members but also contributes to the overall effectiveness and success of the PMO. By investing in the continuous growth of its personnel, a PMO can ensure that it remains adaptive, innovative, and capable of delivering projects that meet organizational goals and stakeholder expectations.

Team Dynamics

Understanding the intricacies of team dynamics is crucial for establishing an effective Project Management Office (PMO). The interplay between team members' roles, communication patterns, and interpersonal relationships can significantly influence the success of a PMO. This subchapter delves into the fundamental aspects of team dynamics, offering insights into how to optimize these elements to create a high-performing PMO.

Firstly, the composition of the team is paramount. A well-balanced team should encompass a diverse mix of skills, experiences, and perspectives. Diversity fosters creativity and innovation, enabling the PMO to tackle complex issues from multiple angles. It is essential to ensure that team members are not only technically proficient but also possess strong soft skills, such as communication, collaboration, and problem-solving abilities. These competencies are vital for fostering a cooperative and productive work environment.

Another critical factor is the establishment of clear roles and responsibilities. Ambiguity in roles can lead to confusion, redundancy, and inefficiencies. A well-defined role structure helps in setting expectations, reducing overlap, and enhancing accountability. Each team member should have a clear understanding of their duties and how they contribute to the overall objectives of the PMO. Regular reviews and updates of these roles can help in adapting to changing project requirements and team dynamics.

Communication is the lifeblood of any successful team. Effective communication strategies should be in place to ensure that information flows seamlessly among team members. This includes regular meetings, progress updates, and open channels for feedback and discussion. Encouraging an open communication culture where team members feel comfortable sharing ideas and concerns can lead to early identification of potential issues and collaborative problem-solving.

Conflict, while often perceived negatively, can be a catalyst for growth and improvement if managed appropriately. Constructive conflict resolution practices should be established to address disagreements and disputes. This involves creating an environment where differing opinions are valued and considered, and where conflicts are addressed promptly and fairly. Techniques such as active listening, mediation, and negotiation can be employed to resolve conflicts and maintain team cohesion.

Trust is a foundational element of effective team dynamics. Building trust within the team involves demonstrating reliability, competence, and integrity. Team leaders play a pivotal role in fostering trust by leading by example, being transparent in their decision-making, and showing genuine concern for their team members' well-being. Trust-building activities, such as team-building exercises and social interactions, can also help in strengthening the bonds among team members.

Leadership within the PMO should be adaptive and responsive to the evolving needs of the team and the projects. Transformational leadership, which focuses on inspiring and motivating team members to achieve their full potential, can be particularly effective in a PMO setting. Leaders should provide a clear vision, set challenging yet attainable goals, and support their team members in achieving these objectives. Regular performance reviews and constructive feedback can help in continuous improvement and professional development.

Incorporating these elements into the team dynamics of a PMO can lead to a more cohesive, efficient, and high-performing team. By focusing on diversity, clear roles, effective communication, constructive conflict resolution, trust-building, and adaptive leadership, a PMO can create an environment conducive to success. Understanding and optimizing team dynamics is not a one-time effort but an ongoing process that requires attention and adjustment as the team and projects evolve.

Leadership and Management

Effective leadership and management within a Project Management Office (PMO) are critical to ensuring its success and sustainability. The distinction between leadership and management is nuanced yet significant. Leadership involves setting a vision, inspiring and motivating the team, while management focuses on planning, organizing, and overseeing processes to achieve the objectives. Both functions are essential for a PMO to operate efficiently and deliver value to the organization.

First, leadership within a PMO requires a clear vision and strategic direction. The PMO leader must articulate the purpose and goals of the PMO, aligning them with the broader organizational objectives. This involves not only understanding the strategic needs of the organization but also communicating this vision effectively to all stakeholders. A PMO leader should possess strong communication skills to convey the vision and motivate the team towards achieving it. This includes fostering a culture of collaboration, innovation, and continuous improvement.

In contrast, management within a PMO involves the practical implementation of the vision through structured processes and methodologies. This includes establishing standardized project management practices, developing and maintaining project documentation, and ensuring that projects are delivered on time, within scope, and on budget. Effective management also requires the ability to allocate resources efficiently, manage risks, and resolve issues promptly. This necessitates a thorough understanding of project management methodologies such as Agile, Scrum, or Waterfall, and the ability to adapt these methodologies to suit the specific needs of the organization.

A critical aspect of both leadership and management is stakeholder engagement. The PMO leader must build strong relationships with key stakeholders, including executive sponsors, project managers, and team members. This involves regular communication and reporting on project progress, as well as soliciting feedback to ensure that the PMO continues to meet the needs of the organization. Effective stakeholder engagement helps to build trust and ensures that the PMO is seen as a valuable asset within the organization.

Another important element is the development and empowerment of the PMO team. Leadership involves mentoring and coaching team members to help them develop their skills and advance their careers. This not only enhances the capabilities of the team but also fosters a sense of loyalty and commitment. Management, on the other hand, involves ensuring that team members have the necessary tools, resources, and training to perform their roles effectively. This includes providing opportunities for professional development and creating an environment where team members feel valued and motivated.

Performance measurement and continuous improvement are also vital. The PMO leader must establish key performance indicators (KPIs) to measure the success of the PMO and its projects. This involves setting clear, measurable goals and regularly reviewing performance against these goals. Management involves using these metrics to identify areas for improvement and implementing changes to enhance efficiency and effectiveness. Continuous improvement is an ongoing process that requires both leadership and management to work together to identify and implement best practices.

Effective leadership and management within a PMO are essential for its success. A PMO leader must balance the visionary aspects of leadership with the practical aspects of management to create a PMO that delivers value to the organization. This involves setting a clear vision, implementing structured processes, engaging stakeholders, developing the team, and continuously measuring and improving performance. By integrating these elements, a PMO can achieve its objectives and contribute significantly to the success of the organization.

Chapter 5: PMO Processes and Methodologies

Standardizing Processes

The establishment of a Project Management Office (PMO) necessitates a robust framework to ensure consistency, efficiency, and effectiveness across all project management activities. A critical component of this framework is the standardization of processes. This involves the development and implementation of uniform procedures and practices that govern how projects are initiated, planned, executed, monitored, and closed. Standardizing processes within a PMO is pivotal for achieving predictable outcomes, optimizing resource utilization, and enhancing overall project performance.

The primary objective of standardizing processes is to create a cohesive environment where project managers and team members operate under a common set of guidelines. This uniformity reduces ambiguity and fosters a shared understanding of project expectations. It also facilitates the seamless transfer of knowledge and skills among team members, thereby enhancing collaboration and reducing the learning curve for new personnel.

A systematic approach to process standardization begins with the identification of key project management processes that require uniformity. These typically include project initiation, planning, execution, monitoring and controlling, and closing. Each of these processes must be meticulously documented, outlining the specific steps, tools, and techniques to be employed. This documentation serves as a reference point for project managers and ensures that all projects adhere to the established standards.

The development of standardized templates and forms is another critical aspect of process standardization. These templates provide a consistent format for project documentation, such as project charters, work breakdown structures (WBS), risk management plans, and status reports. By using standardized templates, project managers can ensure that all necessary information is captured uniformly, facilitating easier review and comparison of projects.

Training and education are essential to the successful implementation of standardized processes. Project managers and team members must be adequately trained on the standardized procedures and the rationale behind them. This training should encompass not only the mechanics of the processes but also the underlying principles of project management that these processes are designed to support.

Regular training sessions and workshops can help reinforce the importance of adherence to standardized processes and allow for the continuous improvement of these processes based on feedback from practitioners.

The role of technology in standardizing processes cannot be overstated. Project management software and tools play a crucial role in ensuring that standardized processes are followed consistently. These tools can automate various aspects of project management, such as scheduling, resource allocation, and progress tracking, thereby reducing the likelihood of deviations from the established procedures. Additionally, they provide a centralized platform for storing and accessing project documentation, ensuring that all team members have access to the most up-to-date information.

Monitoring and evaluation are integral to maintaining the integrity of standardized processes. Regular audits and reviews should be conducted to assess compliance with the standardized procedures and to identify areas for improvement. Metrics and key performance indicators (KPIs) should be established to measure the effectiveness of the standardized processes and their impact on project outcomes. Continuous feedback loops should be implemented to ensure that the processes remain relevant and are adapted to evolving project management practices and organizational needs.

Incorporating standardized processes within a PMO not only enhances operational efficiency but also contributes to the overall maturity of the organization's project management capabilities. By providing a structured approach to managing projects, standardized processes help mitigate risks, improve stakeholder satisfaction, and drive successful project delivery.

Agile vs. Waterfall

The Project Management Office (PMO) plays a pivotal role in standardizing project management practices and optimizing project outcomes. To achieve these objectives, the PMO must navigate through various methodologies that can significantly influence project success. Among the most prominent methodologies are Agile and Waterfall. Both have distinct characteristics, advantages, and limitations, which must be thoroughly understood to make informed decisions on their application within the PMO framework.

Agile methodology is characterized by its iterative and incremental approach. It emphasizes flexibility, customer collaboration, and the ability to respond to change. Agile projects are divided into small, manageable units known as sprints, typically lasting two to four weeks. Each sprint results in a potentially shippable product increment. Key principles of Agile include continuous feedback, adaptive planning, and early delivery of high-value features. This methodology is particularly effective in environments where requirements are expected to evolve or are not well-defined from the outset.

The Agile approach fosters close collaboration between cross-functional teams and stakeholders, ensuring that the final product aligns closely with customer needs. Agile's iterative nature allows for frequent reassessment and adaptation, which can lead to higher customer satisfaction and a reduction in wasted effort. However, Agile requires a high level of discipline, strong team cohesion, and effective communication channels. Without these, the iterative cycles can lead to project delays and scope creep.

In contrast, the Waterfall methodology follows a linear and sequential approach. The project is divided into distinct phases: requirement analysis, system design, implementation, testing, deployment, and maintenance. Each phase must be completed before the next begins, with little room for revisiting previous stages. This structured approach provides clear milestones and deliverables, making it easier to track progress and manage timelines.

Waterfall is advantageous in projects with well-defined requirements and stable environments. It allows for comprehensive documentation and thorough upfront planning, which can mitigate risks and uncertainties. The clear structure facilitates stakeholder understanding and ensures that all project aspects are meticulously addressed before moving forward. However, Waterfall's rigidity can be a drawback in dynamic environments where requirements may change. The inability to accommodate changes without significant rework can lead to project delays and increased costs.

When establishing a PMO, the choice between Agile and Waterfall should be guided by the nature of the projects, organizational culture, and stakeholder expectations. For projects with high uncertainty and evolving requirements, Agile may offer the flexibility needed to adapt and deliver value incrementally. Conversely, for projects with clear, stable requirements and where thorough documentation is critical, Waterfall might be the more suitable approach.

It is also possible for a PMO to adopt a hybrid model, integrating elements of both Agile and Waterfall methodologies. This approach can leverage the strengths of both methodologies, providing the flexibility of Agile while maintaining the structured planning of Waterfall. The hybrid model can be particularly effective in large organizations with diverse project portfolios, allowing the PMO to tailor its approach to the specific needs of each project.

Understanding the fundamental differences between Agile and Waterfall methodologies is crucial for the effective establishment and operation of a PMO. By aligning the chosen methodology with project requirements and organizational goals, the PMO can enhance project delivery, optimize resource utilization, and ultimately drive business success.

Change Management

Change management is a critical component in establishing an effective Project Management Office (PMO). It involves the systematic approach to dealing with the transition or transformation of an organization's goals, processes, or technologies. The objective is to implement strategies for effecting change, controlling change, and helping people adapt to change.

Effective change management requires a thorough understanding of the organizational culture and the specific challenges associated with the change. This begins with a comprehensive assessment of the current state, including identifying potential resistance points and understanding the underlying reasons for resistance. Stakeholder analysis is essential at this stage to categorize stakeholders based on their influence and interest in the PMO's success. This classification helps in formulating targeted communication and engagement strategies.

A clear vision and a well-articulated change strategy are paramount. The vision should convey the benefits of the PMO to the organization, such as improved project success rates, enhanced resource management, and better alignment with business objectives. The strategy should outline the steps needed to achieve this vision, including timelines, resource allocations, and key milestones. It is crucial that this strategy is communicated effectively to all stakeholders to foster buy-in and support.

Leadership plays a pivotal role in change management. Leaders must be visible, accessible, and committed to the change process. Their actions and attitudes set the tone for the rest of the organization. They must also be equipped with the skills to manage resistance and to support their teams through the transition. This may involve training and development programs focused on change management skills, such as communication, conflict resolution, and emotional intelligence.

Communication is another critical element of change management. It must be continuous, transparent, and multi-faceted. Regular updates on the progress of the PMO implementation, successes, and challenges should be shared through various channels, including meetings, emails, newsletters, and intranet postings. Feedback mechanisms should be established to allow employees to voice concerns and provide input, which can then be addressed promptly.

Another important aspect is the management of resistance to change. Resistance can stem from various sources, including fear of the unknown, perceived loss of control, and concerns about competency. Addressing these concerns involves providing adequate training and support, involving employees in the change process, and recognizing and rewarding positive behaviors. It is also beneficial to identify and work with change champions within the organization who can influence their peers and help drive acceptance.

A structured approach to change management also includes the development of a change management plan. This plan should detail the specific actions, timelines, and responsibilities necessary to manage the change process effectively. It should include provisions for monitoring and evaluation to track progress and make adjustments as needed. Metrics and key performance indicators (KPIs) should be defined to measure the impact of the PMO and the effectiveness of the change management efforts.

Incorporating change management into the PMO implementation process ensures that the transition is smooth, and the PMO is positioned for long-term success. It fosters a culture of adaptability and continuous improvement, which is essential for the organization's overall growth and competitiveness. Through careful planning, robust communication, strong leadership, and ongoing support, change management can mitigate risks and enhance the likelihood of achieving the desired outcomes.

Risk Management

Risk management is a critical component in the establishment and operation of an effective Project Management Office (PMO). It involves the systematic identification, assessment, and prioritization of risks followed by coordinated efforts to minimize, monitor, and control the probability or impact of adverse events. Effective risk management ensures that potential problems are addressed proactively, thereby enhancing the probability of project success and organizational resilience.

Central to risk management in a PMO is the development of a comprehensive risk management plan. This plan should outline the methodologies, tools, and techniques that will be employed to manage risks throughout the project lifecycle. It begins with risk identification, where potential risks are recognized and documented. This step involves gathering inputs from various stakeholders, including project team members, customers, and external experts. Techniques such as brainstorming sessions, Delphi technique, SWOT analysis, and checklists are commonly used to uncover potential risks.

Following identification, risk analysis is performed to evaluate the likelihood and impact of each identified risk. This can be achieved through qualitative and quantitative risk analysis methods. Qualitative analysis involves subjective assessment of risks based on their probability and impact, often using a risk matrix to categorize risks into different levels of severity. Quantitative analysis, on the other hand, employs numerical methods such as Monte Carlo simulations, decision tree analysis, and sensitivity analysis to provide a more objective evaluation of risks.

Once risks are analyzed, they must be prioritized to determine which risks require immediate attention and which can be monitored over time. Prioritization is typically based on the combined assessment of risk probability and impact. High-priority risks are those that pose the greatest threat to project objectives and require the most immediate and robust response strategies.

Risk response planning involves developing strategies to mitigate, transfer, accept, or avoid risks. Mitigation efforts aim to reduce the probability or impact of a risk, such as by implementing additional quality checks or increasing resource allocations. Risk transfer involves shifting the impact of a risk to a third party, often through insurance or outsourcing. Acceptance of a risk may be appropriate when the cost of mitigation exceeds the potential impact, and involves developing contingency plans to manage the risk if it materializes. Risk avoidance entails altering project plans to eliminate the risk altogether.

Effective risk management also necessitates continuous monitoring and control of risks throughout the project lifecycle. This involves regular risk assessments, updates to the risk management plan, and communication with stakeholders regarding risk status. Risk audits, status meetings, and risk reviews are essential practices to ensure that risk management activities remain relevant and effective as the project progresses.

Integration of risk management into the PMO's governance framework is vital. This includes establishing clear roles and responsibilities for risk management activities, ensuring that risk management practices are aligned with organizational policies, and fostering a culture of risk awareness and proactive management. Training and development programs should be instituted to enhance the risk management competencies of project managers and team members.

In conclusion, risk management is an indispensable element of a PMO's function, providing a structured approach to identifying, analyzing, and responding to risks. By embedding robust risk management practices within the PMO, organizations can enhance their ability to navigate uncertainties, thereby driving project success and achieving strategic objectives.

Quality Assurance

Quality assurance (QA) in a Project Management Office (PMO) is a critical facet that ensures the delivery of high-quality outcomes aligned with project objectives and organizational standards. Effective QA in a PMO is not merely a series of checks and balances but a systematic approach that integrates quality principles throughout the project lifecycle.

To establish a robust QA framework, the PMO must first define quality standards and metrics that are in alignment with organizational goals. These standards should be documented comprehensively in a quality management plan. The plan serves as a blueprint, detailing the quality objectives, roles and responsibilities, tools, and techniques to be employed, as well as the criteria for quality acceptance.

Quality planning is the initial step in the QA process. It involves identifying the quality requirements and standards for the project and determining how these will be achieved. This phase necessitates collaboration with stakeholders to ensure that their expectations are clearly understood and incorporated into the project deliverables. Effective communication channels must be established to facilitate ongoing dialogue and feedback.

Next, quality assurance activities are integrated into the project processes. This integration is achieved through the implementation of quality audits and process evaluations. Quality audits involve a systematic examination of project activities and processes to ensure compliance with the defined standards. These audits can be conducted internally by the PMO or externally by independent auditors. Process evaluations, on the other hand, focus on the effectiveness and efficiency of the processes in place. They aim to identify areas of improvement and implement corrective actions to enhance process performance.

A key component of QA is continuous monitoring and control. This involves tracking project performance against the quality metrics defined in the quality management plan. Regular quality reviews and inspections are conducted to assess the quality of deliverables and ensure they meet the required standards. Any deviations from the quality standards are documented, and corrective actions are implemented promptly to mitigate any adverse impact on the project.

The PMO should also foster a culture of quality within the project team. This can be achieved through training and development programs that emphasize the importance of quality and equip team members with the necessary skills and knowledge to deliver high-quality outcomes. Encouraging a proactive approach to quality, where team members are empowered to identify and address quality issues, can significantly enhance the overall quality of the project.

Furthermore, the use of quality management tools and techniques is essential for effective QA. Tools such as cause-and-effect diagrams, control charts, and Pareto analysis can help in identifying the root causes of quality issues and implementing effective solutions. These tools provide a data-driven approach to quality management, enabling the PMO to make informed decisions and continuously improve project processes.

Quality assurance is a dynamic and ongoing process that requires commitment and diligence from the entire project team. By embedding quality principles into the project management processes and fostering a culture of continuous improvement, the PMO can ensure that projects are delivered with the highest standards of quality, thereby achieving the desired outcomes and contributing to the overall success of the organization.

Chapter 6: Project Selection and Prioritization

Criteria for Project Selection

Project Management Offices (PMOs) serve as pivotal entities within organizations, orchestrating the alignment of projects with overarching strategic goals. The selection of projects to be managed by a PMO is a critical step that influences the efficacy and success of the PMO itself. Prioritizing projects judiciously ensures that resources are allocated efficiently, risks are mitigated, and benefits are maximized. This subchapter delineates the criteria essential for the selection of projects within the context of establishing an effective PMO.

The first criterion for project selection is strategic alignment. Projects must be evaluated based on their ability to support the organization's strategic objectives. This involves assessing how well a project contributes to the organization's long-term goals and vision. Projects that exhibit a clear alignment with strategic priorities are more likely to receive support and resources, thereby enhancing the overall value delivered by the PMO.

Another crucial criterion is the potential return on investment (ROI). Projects should be scrutinized for their financial viability and potential to generate measurable benefits. This involves calculating the expected costs and benefits associated with a project, including both tangible and intangible factors. Projects with a higher ROI are generally prioritized as they promise greater financial returns and contribute significantly to the organization's growth.

Risk assessment forms a fundamental part of the project selection process. Evaluating the potential risks associated with a project, including technical, financial, and operational risks, is essential. Projects with manageable risk levels and robust risk mitigation strategies are preferred. This ensures that the PMO can effectively oversee the project without encountering unforeseen challenges that could derail the organization's objectives.

Resource availability is another key consideration. The selection of projects should take into account the availability of necessary resources, including personnel, technology, and financial capital. Projects that require resources currently available or those that can be acquired without significant disruption to other operations are more favorable. This criterion ensures that the PMO can execute the project efficiently without overextending the organization's capabilities.

Stakeholder impact is also a vital criterion. Projects should be evaluated based on their potential impact on various stakeholders, including customers, employees, shareholders, and partners. Understanding the stakeholder landscape helps in identifying projects that can garner widespread support and minimize resistance. Projects that positively impact key stakeholders and align with their expectations are more likely to succeed and contribute to the PMO's effectiveness.

Another important criterion is project complexity. Projects with lower complexity levels are often preferred as they are easier to manage and less likely to encounter significant obstacles. However, high-complexity projects that offer substantial strategic benefits or ROI may also be considered, provided there is a clear plan to manage the complexities involved. Balancing project complexity with potential benefits ensures that the PMO can handle the project's demands while still delivering value.

The urgency of the project is another factor to consider. Projects that address immediate organizational needs or capitalize on timely opportunities should be prioritized. This ensures that the PMO is responsive to the dynamic business environment and can leverage opportunities that may not be available in the future.

In sum, the selection of projects for a PMO involves a multifaceted evaluation process. By considering strategic alignment, ROI, risk assessment, resource availability, stakeholder impact, project complexity, and urgency, organizations can ensure that their PMOs manage projects that deliver maximum value and support the achievement of strategic goals. These criteria provide a structured approach to project selection, thereby enhancing the effectiveness and success of the PMO.

Aligning with Strategic Goals

The establishment of a Project Management Office (PMO) is a multifaceted endeavor that necessitates alignment with an organization's overarching strategic goals. This alignment is imperative to ensure that the PMO not only supports but enhances the strategic vision and objectives of the enterprise. To achieve this, it is crucial to first comprehend the strategic goals at a granular level and then map the PMO's functions and initiatives to these goals.

The initial step involves a thorough analysis of the organization's strategic plan. This plan typically encompasses long-term objectives, key performance indicators (KPIs), and the tactical initiatives designed to achieve these goals. Understanding these elements allows the PMO to define its role in facilitating and accelerating strategic success. This requires close collaboration with senior leadership and key stakeholders to ensure that the PMO's mission and objectives are clearly articulated and aligned with the broader organizational strategy.

Once the strategic goals are understood, the PMO must develop a framework that supports these objectives. This framework often includes standardized processes, methodologies, and tools that are designed to enhance project efficiency and effectiveness. For instance, if an organization aims to achieve operational excellence, the PMO might focus on implementing Lean or Six Sigma methodologies to streamline processes and reduce waste. Alternatively, if the strategic goal is innovation and growth, the PMO might prioritize agile methodologies that foster flexibility and rapid iteration.

The alignment process also involves setting up robust governance structures. These structures ensure that projects are selected, prioritized, and executed in a manner that directly contributes to strategic goals. Governance mechanisms such as steering committees, project review boards, and strategic alignment matrices can be employed to maintain this focus. These mechanisms provide oversight and ensure that resources are allocated to projects that offer the highest strategic value.

Metrics and KPIs play a critical role in aligning the PMO with strategic goals. By establishing clear metrics that are directly tied to strategic objectives, the PMO can track progress and demonstrate its impact on the organization's success. These metrics should be integrated into regular reporting and review processes to provide transparency and accountability. Examples of such metrics might include project delivery timelines, budget adherence, and the realization of projected benefits.

Furthermore, the PMO must foster a culture of continuous improvement and strategic alignment. This involves regular training and development programs for PMO staff to ensure they are equipped with the latest skills and knowledge to support strategic initiatives. It also requires periodic reviews of the PMO's processes and methodologies to ensure they remain aligned with evolving strategic goals.

Stakeholder engagement is another critical component. The PMO must actively engage with stakeholders across the organization to understand their needs and ensure that projects are aligned with their expectations. This involves regular communication, feedback loops, and stakeholder involvement in key decision-making processes.

In essence, the alignment of a PMO with strategic goals is an ongoing, dynamic process that requires a deep understanding of the organization's strategic direction, robust governance structures, clear metrics, continuous improvement, and active stakeholder engagement. By meticulously aligning its functions and initiatives with strategic objectives, the PMO can significantly enhance its value proposition and drive organizational success.

Resource Availability

Resource allocation is critical to the success of a Project Management Office (PMO). Ensuring that the necessary resources are available and optimally utilized can significantly influence project outcomes. This chapter examines the various aspects of resource availability, focusing on human resources, financial resources, and technological resources.

Human resources are often the most vital component of any project. When establishing a PMO, it is essential to assess the skills and competencies required for different projects. This involves identifying the current capabilities within the organization and determining any gaps that may exist. Effective resource planning necessitates not only understanding the skill sets of current employees but also forecasting future needs based on the project pipeline. Talent management strategies such as training, development, and recruitment must be employed to bridge any competency gaps. Additionally, maintaining a balanced workload among team members is crucial to prevent burnout and ensure sustained productivity.

Financial resources are another critical factor in the success of a PMO. Budgeting and financial planning are integral to resource management. It is essential to develop a comprehensive financial plan that aligns with the strategic goals of the organization. This plan should include detailed cost estimates for each project, taking into account all potential expenses. Regular financial audits and reviews can help in monitoring expenditures and ensuring that projects remain within budget. It is also important to establish a contingency fund to address any unforeseen financial challenges that may arise during the project lifecycle.

Technological resources play a pivotal role in the efficient functioning of a PMO. The selection of appropriate project management tools and software can greatly enhance the ability to plan, execute, and monitor projects. These tools facilitate better communication, collaboration, and documentation, thereby improving overall project efficiency. It is important to evaluate the technological needs of the PMO and invest in tools that offer scalability and integration with existing systems. Regular training sessions should be conducted to ensure that all team members are proficient in using these tools.

The availability of resources is influenced by several external and internal factors. External factors such as market conditions, economic climate, and regulatory changes can impact resource availability. Internally, organizational policies, corporate culture, and strategic priorities play a significant role. It is important to conduct a thorough analysis of these factors to understand their potential impact on resource availability. This analysis can help in developing strategies to mitigate any adverse effects and ensure a steady supply of resources.

Effective communication is essential for resource management. Clear and transparent communication channels must be established to ensure that all stakeholders are aware of resource availability and any potential constraints. Regular meetings and updates can help in identifying any issues early and taking corrective actions. It is also important to foster a culture of collaboration and teamwork, where all team members are encouraged to share their insights and contribute to resource planning.

In conclusion, resource availability is a multifaceted aspect of PMO management that requires careful planning and continuous monitoring. By effectively managing human, financial, and technological resources, a PMO can significantly enhance its ability to deliver successful projects. Adopting a proactive approach to resource management, supported by clear communication and strategic planning, can help in overcoming challenges and achieving organizational goals.

Balancing Short-term and Long-term Projects

Effective project management requires a nuanced approach to balancing short-term and long-term projects. This balance is pivotal for the success of a Project Management Office (PMO). Short-term projects typically focus on immediate objectives and deliverables, whereas long-term projects are concerned with strategic goals and sustainable outcomes. The alignment of these two types of projects is critical for the overall health and efficiency of an organization.

Short-term projects often demand rapid execution and tangible results. They are characterized by shorter timelines, specific deliverables, and immediate resource allocation. These projects are essential for maintaining operational momentum and addressing urgent business needs. They provide quick wins that can boost team morale and demonstrate the value of the PMO to stakeholders. However, an excessive focus on short-term projects can lead to resource depletion and strategic myopia.

Long-term projects, on the other hand, are designed to achieve broader organizational goals. These projects typically span multiple quarters or years and involve significant planning, resource allocation, and risk management. They are crucial for driving innovation, achieving strategic objectives, and ensuring the long-term sustainability of the organization. The primary challenge with long-term projects is maintaining stakeholder engagement and resource commitment over extended periods.

To balance short-term and long-term projects effectively, PMOs must implement a structured portfolio management approach. This involves categorizing projects based on their timelines, objectives, and strategic importance. A well-defined project portfolio allows PMOs to allocate resources efficiently, prioritize tasks, and ensure that both short-term and long-term projects receive adequate attention.

Resource allocation is a critical aspect of balancing these projects. PMOs must develop a resource management framework that identifies the availability and capacity of resources, including personnel, budget, and technology. This framework should allow for dynamic resource reallocation based on project priorities and changing organizational needs. Effective resource management ensures that short-term projects do not cannibalize resources needed for long-term initiatives and vice versa.

Risk management is another essential component. Short-term projects often face operational risks, such as tight deadlines and limited scope changes. Long-term projects, however, are more susceptible to strategic risks, including market shifts, technological advancements, and regulatory changes. PMOs must establish a comprehensive risk management strategy that addresses both types of risks. This strategy should include regular risk assessments, contingency planning, and proactive mitigation measures.

Communication plays a pivotal role in maintaining a balance between short-term and long-term projects. Clear and consistent communication ensures that all stakeholders are aware of project statuses, priorities, and challenges. Regular updates and transparent reporting mechanisms help in managing expectations and securing ongoing support for both types of projects. Engaging stakeholders through effective communication fosters collaboration and alignment with organizational goals.

Performance measurement is equally important. PMOs should establish key performance indicators (KPIs) that reflect the success of both short-term and long-term projects. These KPIs should be aligned with organizational objectives and provide insights into project performance, resource utilization, and strategic alignment. Regular performance reviews enable PMOs to make informed decisions and adjustments to the project portfolio as needed.

Incorporating flexibility into project planning and execution is also vital. The dynamic nature of business environments requires PMOs to be adaptable and responsive. Agile methodologies and iterative processes can be beneficial in managing both short-term and long-term projects. These approaches allow for continuous improvement, rapid response to changes, and enhanced stakeholder engagement.

Balancing short-term and long-term projects within a PMO framework is a complex but essential task. By implementing structured portfolio management, efficient resource allocation, comprehensive risk management, clear communication, and performance measurement, PMOs can achieve a harmonious balance that drives organizational success.

Review and Approval Process

The establishment of an effective Project Management Office (PMO) necessitates a meticulous review and approval process. This process ensures that all projects align with organizational goals, adhere to established standards, and utilize resources efficiently. The review and approval process typically involves several stages, each of which plays a critical role in maintaining the integrity and effectiveness of the PMO.

Initially, project proposals undergo a preliminary review. This stage involves evaluating the project's alignment with strategic objectives, its feasibility, and its potential impact on the organization. Key stakeholders, including senior management and the PMO director, assess the proposal's relevance and the anticipated benefits. This step ensures that only projects with a clear strategic fit progress to the next stage.

Following the preliminary review, a detailed project assessment is conducted. This assessment includes a thorough analysis of the project's scope, timeline, budget, and resource requirements. Subject matter experts and project managers collaborate to scrutinize the project's technical aspects and risk factors. The assessment aims to identify potential challenges and devise mitigation strategies, ensuring that the project is viable and sustainable.

Once the detailed assessment is complete, the project proposal is subjected to a formal approval process. This involves presenting the project plan to an approval committee, which typically comprises senior executives, financial officers, and key stakeholders. The committee reviews the project's strategic alignment, financial implications, and resource allocation. They also consider the project's risk profile and the proposed mitigation measures. The approval committee's role is to provide an objective evaluation and ensure that the project aligns with the organization's overall strategy and resource capabilities.

If the project receives approval, it progresses to the planning and execution phase. However, the review and approval process does not end here. Continuous monitoring and periodic reviews are integral to maintaining project alignment and performance. The PMO establishes key performance indicators (KPIs) and milestones to track the project's progress. Regular status reports and review meetings are conducted to assess the project's adherence to the plan, budget, and timeline. These reviews allow for timely identification of deviations and implementation of corrective actions.

In cases where projects do not meet the required standards during the review stages, they may be revised or rejected. Feedback from the review process provides valuable insights for refining project proposals. This iterative process helps in enhancing the quality of future project submissions and fosters a culture of continuous improvement within the organization.

Effective communication is crucial throughout the review and approval process. Clear and transparent communication ensures that all stakeholders are informed about the project's status, decisions made, and any changes in scope or direction. The

PMO facilitates this communication through regular updates, meetings, and documentation.

The review and approval process is a cornerstone of an effective PMO. It ensures that projects are strategically aligned, feasible, and well-planned. By implementing a rigorous review and approval process, organizations can optimize resource utilization, minimize risks, and achieve their strategic objectives. The process also fosters accountability and transparency, contributing to the overall success and sustainability of the PMO.

Chapter 7: Implementing PMO Tools

Project Management Software

Project management software plays a pivotal role in establishing and operating an effective Project Management Office (PMO). These digital tools provide a structured framework for planning, executing, and monitoring projects, thereby enhancing the efficiency and effectiveness of project management activities. The integration of software solutions in PMO operations can significantly streamline workflows, improve collaboration, and ensure alignment with organizational goals.

One of the primary benefits of project management software is its ability to centralize project data. By consolidating information in a single repository, these tools facilitate easy access to project plans, schedules, resource allocations, and progress reports. This centralization minimizes the risk of data silos and ensures that all stakeholders have access to up-to-date information, which is crucial for informed decision-making. Additionally, centralized data storage enhances transparency and accountability, as project managers can easily track and document changes, issues, and milestones.

Another critical advantage is the automation of routine tasks. Project management software can automate various administrative functions such as task assignments, notifications, and reporting. Automation reduces the manual effort required for these activities, allowing project managers to focus on more strategic aspects of project management. For instance, automated scheduling tools can generate project timelines based on predefined parameters, thus reducing the likelihood of scheduling conflicts and delays.

Collaboration is a cornerstone of successful project management, and software tools are instrumental in facilitating effective communication among team members. Features such as shared workspaces, real-time messaging, and document sharing enable teams to collaborate seamlessly, regardless of their geographical locations. This capability is particularly beneficial in today's globalized work environment, where remote and distributed teams are increasingly common. Enhanced collaboration tools also support better stakeholder engagement by providing platforms for feedback, discussions, and approvals.

Resource management is another critical area where project management software can provide substantial benefits. These tools offer functionalities for resource planning, allocation, and tracking, ensuring that resources are optimally utilized throughout the project lifecycle. Advanced software solutions can also provide predictive analytics to forecast resource needs and potential bottlenecks, thereby enabling proactive management of resources. This level of foresight is invaluable for maintaining project timelines and budgets.

Risk management is an integral component of project management, and software solutions offer robust features for identifying, assessing, and mitigating risks. These tools can generate risk matrices, track risk mitigation activities, and provide real-time updates on risk status. By systematically managing risks, PMOs can enhance their ability to deliver projects successfully and reduce the likelihood of unforeseen issues derailing project objectives.

The integration of project management software with other organizational systems, such as Enterprise Resource Planning (ERP) and Customer Relationship Management (CRM) systems, further amplifies its benefits. This integration ensures a seamless flow of information across different functional areas, promoting a holistic approach to project management. For example, integrating project management software with financial systems can provide real-time insights into project costs and financial performance, enabling better budget management and financial forecasting.

In conclusion, project management software is an indispensable tool for any PMO aiming to improve its operational efficiency and project delivery capabilities. The functionalities offered by these tools, including data centralization, task automation, enhanced collaboration, resource management, risk management, and system integration, collectively contribute to a more streamlined and effective project management process. As technology continues to evolve, the capabilities of project management software will undoubtedly expand, offering even greater potential for optimizing PMO performance.

Collaboration Tools

Establishing an effective Project Management Office (PMO) necessitates the integration of robust collaboration tools to streamline communication, enhance productivity, and ensure seamless project execution. These tools serve as the backbone of a PMO, enabling team members to coordinate tasks, share information, and monitor progress efficiently. The selection and implementation of appropriate collaboration tools are critical for the success of any PMO.

One of the primary categories of collaboration tools includes project management software. These platforms, such as Microsoft Project, Asana, and Trello, provide comprehensive solutions for task assignment, scheduling, and resource allocation. They facilitate real-time updates, allowing team members to track project milestones and deadlines effectively. The visual representation of tasks and timelines through Gantt charts and Kanban boards aids in better understanding and management of project workflows.

Communication tools are equally vital in fostering collaboration within a PMO. Platforms like Slack, Microsoft Teams, and Zoom offer various functionalities that support instant messaging, video conferencing, and file sharing. These tools bridge geographical and temporal gaps, ensuring that team members can communicate and collaborate regardless of their location. The integration of these tools with other project management software further enhances their utility, allowing for seamless information flow and reducing the risk of miscommunication.

Document management systems (DMS) play a crucial role in maintaining the integrity and accessibility of project documentation. Tools such as SharePoint, Google Drive, and Dropbox provide centralized repositories for storing, organizing, and sharing documents. They offer version control features, ensuring that team members are always working with the most up-to-date information. The ability to set permissions and access levels within these systems ensures that sensitive information is protected while still being accessible to authorized personnel.

Time tracking and reporting tools are essential for monitoring project progress and ensuring accountability. Tools like Toggl, Harvest, and Clockify allow team members to log their hours and track the time spent on various tasks. These tools generate detailed reports that provide insights into productivity and resource utilization, enabling PMO leaders to make data-driven decisions. The integration of time tracking tools with project management software further streamlines the process of monitoring and reporting.

Collaboration tools also include platforms for stakeholder engagement and feedback collection. Tools such as SurveyMonkey, Typeform, and JotForm facilitate the creation and distribution of surveys and questionnaires. These tools enable the PMO to gather valuable input from stakeholders, ensuring that their needs and expectations are met. The analysis of survey data provides insights that can inform project planning and execution.

Security and compliance tools are indispensable in ensuring that the PMO adheres to industry standards and regulations. Tools like Symantec, McAfee, and Norton provide comprehensive security solutions that protect sensitive project data from cyber threats. Compliance management software, such as LogicGate and VComply, helps the PMO maintain adherence to regulatory requirements, reducing the risk of legal and financial repercussions.

The integration and effective use of these collaboration tools require a strategic approach. PMO leaders must assess the specific needs of their teams and projects to select the most appropriate tools. Training and ongoing support are essential to ensure that team members can utilize these tools effectively. Regular evaluation and updates to the toolset are necessary to keep pace with technological advancements and evolving project demands.

Incorporating collaboration tools into the PMO framework not only enhances efficiency and productivity but also fosters a culture of transparency and accountability. The ability to communicate, share information, and track progress in real-time empowers team members to contribute effectively to project success.

Reporting and Analytics

In the realm of Project Management Offices (PMOs), the capacity to harness data for informed decision-making is paramount. Effective reporting and analytics serve as the cornerstone for this capability, enabling PMOs to deliver actionable insights, monitor performance, and drive strategic initiatives. This subchapter elucidates the methodologies, tools, and best practices essential for establishing robust reporting and analytics frameworks within a PMO.

A foundational aspect of reporting within a PMO is the identification and standardization of key performance indicators (KPIs). These metrics should align with the organization's strategic objectives and encompass various dimensions of project performance, including scope, time, cost, quality, and risk. The selection of KPIs necessitates a thorough understanding of stakeholder requirements and the specific goals of the PMO. Once established, these KPIs provide a basis for consistent and objective performance assessment.

The architecture of an effective reporting system hinges on the integration of data from multiple sources. This often involves deploying sophisticated project management information systems (PMIS) that facilitate real-time data collection, processing, and dissemination. The PMIS should support seamless integration with other enterprise systems, such as financial and human resource management platforms, to ensure comprehensive and accurate data capture. The deployment of these systems must be accompanied by rigorous data governance policies to maintain data quality and integrity.

Advanced analytics capabilities, including predictive and prescriptive analytics, can significantly enhance the PMO's ability to anticipate and mitigate potential issues. Predictive analytics leverages historical data to forecast future project performance and identify trends that may impact project outcomes. Prescriptive analytics, on the other hand, provides recommendations for optimizing project strategies and resource allocation based on predictive insights. The implementation of these advanced analytics techniques requires a combination of statistical expertise and domain knowledge to interpret results accurately and translate them into actionable strategies.

Visualization tools play a critical role in the communication of analytical insights. Effective visualizations transform complex data sets into intuitive and easily digestible formats, facilitating better understanding and decision-making among stakeholders. Dashboards, heat maps, and Gantt charts are common visualization tools that provide real-time visibility into project performance. The design of these visualizations should prioritize clarity, relevance, and accessibility, ensuring that stakeholders at all levels can derive value from the presented data.

Continuous improvement in reporting and analytics is achieved through regular feedback loops and iterative refinement. Stakeholder feedback is invaluable in assessing the effectiveness of existing reports and identifying areas for enhancement. Additionally, benchmarking against industry standards and best practices can provide insights into emerging trends and innovative approaches that can be adopted to elevate the PMO's reporting capabilities.

The ethical considerations of data usage within the PMO context must also be addressed. Ensuring data privacy and security is paramount, particularly when dealing with sensitive project information. Compliance with relevant regulations and standards, such as GDPR or ISO 27001, is essential to safeguard against data breaches and maintain stakeholder trust.

In summary, the establishment of a robust reporting and analytics framework within a PMO is a multifaceted endeavor that requires careful planning, integration, and continuous enhancement. By leveraging advanced analytics, standardized KPIs, and effective visualization tools, PMOs can significantly enhance their ability to deliver value, drive strategic initiatives, and achieve organizational objectives. The continuous evolution of these practices, guided by stakeholder feedback and industry benchmarks, will ensure that the PMO remains at the forefront of data-driven decision-making in project management.

Integration with Existing Systems

Effective integration of a Project Management Office (PMO) with existing systems is paramount for achieving streamlined operations and enhanced project outcomes. This process necessitates a thorough understanding of both the PMO's objectives and the current technological landscape within the organization. A methodical approach ensures that the PMO not only complements but also optimizes the existing infrastructure, fostering a cohesive environment for project management.

The first step in this integration involves a comprehensive assessment of the existing systems. This includes project management software, enterprise resource planning (ERP) systems, customer relationship management (CRM) platforms, and any other tools currently in use. Understanding their functionalities, data flows, and user interfaces is critical. This assessment helps identify potential redundancies, gaps, and opportunities for enhancement. Key stakeholders, including IT personnel, project managers, and end-users, should be engaged in this process to provide insights and feedback.

Once the assessment is complete, the next phase involves defining the integration requirements. These requirements should align with the PMO's objectives, such as improving project tracking, enhancing resource allocation, and ensuring real-time reporting. Clear and detailed requirements facilitate the selection of appropriate integration methods and tools. It is essential to prioritize these requirements based on their impact on project efficiency and organizational goals.

Selecting the right integration tools and technologies is crucial. Middleware solutions, Application Programming Interfaces (APIs), and integration platforms as a service (iPaaS) are commonly used to connect disparate systems. The choice of tool depends on factors such as compatibility with existing systems, scalability, ease of use, and cost. It is advisable to conduct a pilot test with a limited scope to evaluate the tool's effectiveness and identify any potential issues before full-scale implementation.

Data synchronization is a critical aspect of system integration. Ensuring that data is accurately and consistently shared between the PMO and existing systems prevents discrepancies and enhances decision-making. This involves establishing data mapping protocols, defining data ownership, and setting up automated data transfer mechanisms. Regular audits and monitoring are necessary to maintain data integrity and address any synchronization issues promptly.

User training and change management play a pivotal role in the successful integration of a PMO with existing systems. Users must be adequately trained on new processes, tools, and workflows to ensure seamless adoption. Change management strategies, including clear communication, stakeholder engagement, and support mechanisms, help mitigate resistance and foster a positive attitude towards the integration.

Ongoing evaluation and optimization are essential to maintain the effectiveness of the integrated systems. Regular reviews should be conducted to assess the performance of the integration, identify any areas for improvement, and implement necessary adjustments. Feedback from users and stakeholders should be continuously gathered and analyzed to inform these evaluations.

Incorporating a PMO into an organization's existing systems can significantly enhance project management capabilities. However, it requires a structured approach, from initial assessment and requirement definition to tool selection, data synchronization, user training, and ongoing evaluation. By meticulously planning and executing each step, organizations can achieve a harmonious integration that leverages the strengths of both the PMO and the existing systems, ultimately leading to improved project outcomes and organizational efficiency.

Training and Support

The establishment of a Project Management Office (PMO) necessitates a comprehensive strategy for training and support to ensure its successful implementation and sustainability. Training and support are pivotal elements that bridge the gap between theoretical frameworks and practical application, fostering a culture of continuous improvement and proficiency in project management practices.

Training programs should be meticulously designed to address the specific needs of the organization and the skill levels of its personnel. Initial training must encompass fundamental project management principles, methodologies, and tools, ensuring that all team members possess a baseline understanding. Advanced training modules should be tailored to enhance the competencies of project managers and PMO staff, focusing on specialized areas such as risk management, stakeholder engagement, and advanced project analytics.

The modes of training delivery are crucial in maximizing the absorption and retention of knowledge. A blended learning approach, combining face-to-face workshops, online courses, and interactive simulations, can cater to diverse learning preferences and schedules. Workshops and seminars facilitate hands-on experience and real-time problem-solving, while e-learning modules offer flexibility and self-paced learning opportunities. Simulation exercises, replicating real-world project scenarios, allow participants to apply theoretical knowledge in a controlled environment, thereby reinforcing learning outcomes.

Support mechanisms are equally vital in the operational phase of the PMO. A robust support framework includes access to resources, ongoing mentorship, and a feedback loop to continuously refine processes. Establishing a knowledge repository, populated with templates, guidelines, and best practices, provides a valuable reference for project teams. This repository should be dynamic, regularly updated to reflect emerging trends and lessons learned from completed projects.

Mentorship programs contribute significantly to the professional development of PMO staff and project managers. Pairing less experienced personnel with seasoned mentors facilitates knowledge transfer and offers personalized guidance. These mentor-mentee relationships encourage the sharing of tacit knowledge, which is often not captured in formal training sessions. Regular check-ins and progress reviews ensure that mentees are on track and can address any challenges they encounter.

A feedback mechanism is essential for continuous improvement and adaptation. Regular surveys and feedback sessions with project teams and stakeholders can identify areas of improvement and highlight successful practices. This feedback should be systematically analyzed and used to refine training programs and support structures. Incorporating feedback loops ensures that the PMO evolves in alignment with organizational needs and external project management advancements.

To maintain the relevance and effectiveness of training and support initiatives, it is imperative to stay abreast of industry developments and emerging best practices. Participation in professional networks, conferences, and certification programs can provide valuable insights and foster a culture of lifelong learning within the PMO. Encouraging PMO staff to attain recognized certifications, such as PMP (Project Management Professional) or PRINCE2 (Projects IN Controlled Environments), enhances their credibility and ensures adherence to globally accepted standards.

In summary, the integration of comprehensive training and robust support mechanisms is critical to the successful establishment and ongoing efficacy of a PMO. By investing in continuous education and fostering a supportive environment, organizations can enhance their project management capabilities, leading to improved project outcomes and strategic alignment.

Chapter 8: Change Management in PMO

Understanding Change Management

Change management is a critical aspect of establishing an effective Project Management Office (PMO). It involves a systematic approach to dealing with the transition or transformation of an organization's goals, processes, or technologies. The primary objective is to implement strategies for effecting change, controlling change, and helping people adapt to change. Effective change management enhances the success rate of projects and initiatives by ensuring minimal disruption to operations and maximizing the benefits of the change.

Change management encompasses several key components, including understanding the need for change, planning for change, implementing change, and sustaining change. Each of these components involves distinct activities and requires careful consideration to ensure successful outcomes.

Understanding the need for change involves identifying the drivers that necessitate change. These drivers can be internal, such as operational inefficiencies, or external, such as market competition or regulatory requirements. Conducting a thorough analysis of these drivers helps in articulating a clear and compelling case for change, which is crucial for gaining stakeholder buy-in and support.

Planning for change involves developing a comprehensive change management strategy. This strategy should outline the vision for change, the objectives to be achieved, and the steps necessary to achieve these objectives. It should also include a risk management plan to identify potential obstacles and develop mitigation strategies. Effective communication is a critical element of the planning phase. Clear, consistent, and transparent communication helps to manage expectations, reduce uncertainty, and build trust among stakeholders.

Implementing change involves executing the change management plan. This phase requires careful coordination and collaboration among various stakeholders. It may involve training programs to equip employees with the necessary skills and knowledge, restructuring organizational processes, or deploying new technologies. Monitoring and evaluation are essential during the implementation phase to ensure that the change is progressing as planned and to make necessary adjustments.

Sustaining change involves embedding the changes into the organizational culture and practices to ensure long-term success. This requires continuous reinforcement of the new behaviors and practices through regular feedback, recognition, and rewards. Leadership plays a crucial role in sustaining change by demonstrating commitment to the change and modeling the desired behaviors. Additionally, establishing mechanisms for continuous improvement can help in identifying and addressing any emerging issues, thereby ensuring the change remains effective and relevant.

Resistance to change is a common challenge in change management. Understanding the sources of resistance, such as fear of the unknown, loss of control, or perceived negative impacts, is crucial for developing effective strategies to address them. Engaging stakeholders early and often, providing adequate support and resources, and involving employees in the change process can help mitigate resistance and foster a positive attitude towards change.

Incorporating change management into the PMO framework enhances the organization's ability to adapt to changing environments and achieve strategic objectives. It ensures that changes are implemented in a structured and systematic manner, minimizing disruptions and maximizing benefits. By understanding and effectively managing change, organizations can improve their project success rates, increase employee engagement, and drive sustainable growth.

Communication Strategies

Effective communication is a cornerstone for the successful implementation and operation of a Project Management Office (PMO). A well-structured communication strategy ensures that all stakeholders are aligned, informed, and engaged throughout the project lifecycle. To achieve this, it is essential to establish clear communication channels, utilize appropriate tools, and maintain transparency in all interactions.

Firstly, identifying the key stakeholders and understanding their communication needs is crucial. Stakeholders can include project sponsors, team members, clients, and other departments within the organization. Each group may require different levels of detail and frequency of updates. For instance, senior management might need high-level summaries, while project teams may require detailed task-specific information. Tailoring the communication approach to the audience ensures that the information provided is relevant and useful.

The selection of communication channels plays a significant role in the effectiveness of the PMO. Traditional methods such as face-to-face meetings, emails, and reports remain valuable, but modern tools like project management software, instant messaging platforms, and video conferencing can enhance real-time collaboration and information sharing. Utilizing a mix of these channels can cater to different preferences and situations. For example, regular face-to-face meetings can be complemented by instant messaging for quick queries and project management software for tracking progress and sharing documents.

Regular and structured communication is essential to keep all parties informed and engaged. Establishing a communication plan that outlines the frequency, format, and responsible parties for each type of communication can provide clarity and consistency. This plan should include regular status updates, milestone reviews, and ad-hoc communications for urgent issues. Consistent communication helps in managing expectations, identifying potential issues early, and ensuring that everyone is on the same page.

Transparency in communication fosters trust and collaboration among stakeholders. Sharing both successes and challenges openly can create a culture of honesty and accountability. This involves not only reporting on project progress but also discussing risks, issues, and any changes to the project scope or timeline. Transparent communication allows for collective problem-solving and ensures that stakeholders are prepared for any eventualities.

Feedback mechanisms are a vital component of a robust communication strategy. Encouraging stakeholders to provide feedback on communication processes and the information shared can help in continuously improving the effectiveness of communication. This can be achieved through regular surveys, feedback sessions, and open forums. Acting on the feedback received demonstrates a commitment to continuous improvement and responsiveness to stakeholder needs.

Another critical aspect is the documentation of all communications. Keeping detailed records of meetings, decisions, and communications ensures that there is a clear historical record that can be referred to if needed. This can help in resolving disputes, tracking decisions, and ensuring accountability. Proper documentation also aids in the onboarding of new team members and stakeholders by providing them with comprehensive background information.

Lastly, training and development in communication skills can greatly enhance the effectiveness of the PMO. Providing training sessions on effective communication techniques, tools, and best practices can equip team members with the skills they need to communicate effectively. This can include training on active listening, clear and concise writing, and effective presentation skills.

In conclusion, a well-defined communication strategy is essential for the success of a PMO. By understanding stakeholder needs, choosing appropriate communication channels, maintaining regular and transparent communication, incorporating feedback, documenting communications, and providing training, a PMO can ensure that all stakeholders are informed, engaged, and aligned towards achieving project goals.

Stakeholder Engagement

Effective stakeholder engagement is a critical component in the establishment and operation of a successful Project Management Office (PMO). Stakeholders, encompassing a wide array of individuals and groups including executive leadership, project managers, team members, clients, and external partners, play a pivotal role in shaping the objectives, strategies, and outcomes of the PMO. Their active involvement and support are essential for aligning the PMO's goals with organizational priorities and ensuring the successful execution of projects.

Identifying stakeholders is the first step in the engagement process. It requires a comprehensive understanding of the organizational structure and the various interests and influences of different individuals and groups. Stakeholders can be categorized based on their level of influence and interest in the PMO's activities. High-influence stakeholders, such as executive sponsors and department heads, require particular attention, as their support can significantly impact the PMO's success. Conversely, stakeholders with lower influence but high interest, such as team members and end-users, provide valuable insights and feedback that can enhance project outcomes.

Once stakeholders are identified, the next step involves analyzing their needs and expectations. This can be accomplished through various methods such as surveys, interviews, and workshops. Understanding stakeholders' perspectives helps in tailoring communication and engagement strategies to address their concerns and requirements effectively. It is crucial to establish clear communication channels and maintain transparency in all PMO activities to build trust and foster a collaborative environment.

Stakeholder engagement strategies should be designed to promote continuous interaction and feedback. Regular meetings, status updates, and progress reports are essential tools for keeping stakeholders informed and involved. These interactions provide opportunities to address any issues or concerns promptly and to make necessary adjustments to project plans. Additionally, involving stakeholders in decision-making processes, especially in critical phases of project planning and execution, ensures their buy-in and commitment to the project's success.

Effective communication is at the heart of stakeholder engagement. It is important to tailor communication styles and methods to suit the preferences and needs of different stakeholders. For instance, executive leadership may prefer high-level summaries and strategic insights, while project teams might require detailed technical information. Utilizing a mix of communication tools such as emails, meetings, dashboards, and collaboration platforms can cater to diverse communication needs and enhance overall engagement.

Monitoring and evaluating stakeholder engagement efforts is essential to ensure their effectiveness. This involves regularly assessing stakeholder satisfaction and the impact of engagement activities on project outcomes. Feedback mechanisms should be in place to gather stakeholders' opinions and suggestions, which can be used to refine engagement strategies continually. Metrics such as stakeholder satisfaction scores, participation rates in meetings and workshops, and the frequency of communication can provide valuable insights into the effectiveness of engagement efforts.

Building strong relationships with stakeholders is a continuous process that extends beyond the lifecycle of individual projects. It involves nurturing trust, demonstrating value, and maintaining open lines of communication. By prioritizing stakeholder engagement, the PMO can create a supportive environment that facilitates project success and drives organizational growth.

Stakeholder engagement is not a one-time activity but an ongoing commitment that requires strategic planning, effective communication, and regular evaluation. By integrating these principles into the PMO's operations, organizations can enhance stakeholder satisfaction, improve project outcomes, and achieve long-term success.

Monitoring and Evaluation

Monitoring and evaluation (M&E) are pivotal components in the establishment and operation of an effective Project Management Office (PMO). These processes ensure that project activities align with strategic objectives, resources are utilized efficiently, and desired outcomes are achieved. Effective M&E frameworks provide continuous feedback, facilitating timely adjustments and fostering a culture of accountability and continuous improvement within the PMO.

The monitoring process involves the systematic collection, analysis, and use of information to track project performance against predefined criteria. Key performance indicators (KPIs) serve as benchmarks for assessing progress. These indicators should be specific, measurable, achievable, relevant, and time-bound (SMART). Regular data collection through project management tools and techniques, such as Gantt charts, dashboards, and status reports, enables the PMO to maintain an up-to-date understanding of project status.

Evaluation, on the other hand, is a periodic assessment that examines the relevance, effectiveness, efficiency, impact, and sustainability of project outcomes. It is typically conducted at key milestones or project completion. Evaluation methods may include qualitative and quantitative approaches, such as surveys, interviews, focus groups, and statistical analysis. The insights gained from evaluations inform decision-making and strategic planning, ensuring that the PMO remains aligned with organizational goals.

To implement an effective M&E system, the PMO must first establish a clear framework outlining the objectives, scope, and methodology of monitoring and evaluation activities. This framework should be integrated into the overall project management plan and communicated to all stakeholders to ensure transparency and buy-in. It is essential to define roles and responsibilities for M&E activities, designating specific team members or external experts to oversee data collection, analysis, and reporting.

Data integrity is crucial for the reliability of M&E outcomes. The PMO should implement robust data management practices, including standardized data collection procedures, regular data quality checks, and secure data storage. Leveraging technology, such as project management software and data analytics tools, can enhance the efficiency and accuracy of data collection and analysis processes.

Stakeholder involvement is another critical aspect of effective M&E. Engaging stakeholders, including project team members, sponsors, and beneficiaries, in the M&E process ensures that diverse perspectives are considered and that the findings are relevant and actionable. Regular communication and feedback loops between the PMO and stakeholders help to build trust and promote a shared understanding of project performance and outcomes.

Continuous improvement is a fundamental principle of effective M&E. The PMO should utilize M&E findings to identify lessons learned and best practices, which can be applied to future projects. This iterative process of learning and adaptation helps to refine project management methodologies and enhance the overall performance of the PMO.

In conclusion, monitoring and evaluation are integral to the success of a PMO. By systematically tracking project performance and assessing outcomes, the PMO can ensure that projects deliver value and contribute to the achievement of organizational objectives. Establishing a robust M&E framework, maintaining data integrity, engaging stakeholders, and fostering continuous improvement are key elements in creating an effective PMO.

Sustaining Change

The establishment of a Project Management Office (PMO) is a significant endeavor, but ensuring its long-term success requires a strategic approach to sustaining change. The initial implementation phase often garners enthusiasm and momentum, yet it is the ongoing commitment to continuous improvement and adaptation that solidifies the PMO's role within an organization.

A critical factor in sustaining change is the integration of the PMO into the broader organizational culture. This involves aligning the PMO's objectives with the strategic goals of the company and ensuring that it is perceived as a valuable asset rather than an external entity. To achieve this, leadership must consistently communicate the benefits and successes of the PMO, thereby fostering a sense of ownership and support among stakeholders at all levels.

Another essential element is the establishment of robust governance structures. Effective governance provides the framework for decision-making, accountability, and performance monitoring. Regular reviews and audits of PMO processes and outcomes help maintain alignment with organizational priorities and identify areas for improvement. This iterative feedback loop ensures that the PMO remains responsive to changing business needs and continues to deliver value.

The PMO must also invest in the development of its personnel. Continuous professional development and training programs are vital for maintaining high standards of project management practice. By equipping team members with the latest tools, techniques, and methodologies, the PMO can adapt to new challenges and innovations in the field. Additionally, fostering a culture of knowledge sharing and collaboration within the PMO and across the organization enhances overall project performance and drives continuous improvement.

Technology plays a pivotal role in sustaining the effectiveness of a PMO. Leveraging advanced project management software and tools can streamline processes, enhance data accuracy, and improve communication. The adoption of digital dashboards and real-time reporting systems enables more informed decision-making and provides transparency into project progress and performance metrics. However, it is crucial to regularly evaluate and update technological solutions to ensure they meet the evolving needs of the PMO and the organization.

Stakeholder engagement is another cornerstone of sustained PMO success. Regular communication with key stakeholders, including project sponsors, team members, and end-users, ensures that their needs and expectations are understood and addressed. Feedback mechanisms, such as surveys and focus groups, provide valuable insights into stakeholder perceptions and areas for enhancement. By actively involving stakeholders in the PMO's activities and decision-making processes, the organization can build stronger relationships and foster a collaborative environment.

Moreover, the PMO should adopt a proactive approach to risk management. Identifying potential risks early and developing mitigation strategies can prevent disruptions and ensure the continuity of project activities. This includes conducting regular risk assessments, maintaining a risk register, and fostering a risk-aware culture within the project teams. By anticipating and addressing challenges before they escalate, the PMO can maintain stability and resilience.

In conclusion, sustaining change within a PMO requires a multifaceted approach that encompasses cultural integration, robust governance, continuous development, technological advancement, stakeholder engagement, and proactive risk management. By focusing on these areas, organizations can ensure that their PMO remains a dynamic and effective component of their project management strategy, capable of adapting to new challenges and driving long-term success.

Chapter 9: PMO Governance

Establishing Governance Policies

The establishment of governance policies within a Project Management Office (PMO) is a critical step towards ensuring effective project oversight and alignment with organizational goals. Governance policies provide a structured framework that delineates the roles, responsibilities, procedures, and standards necessary for the PMO to function optimally. The formulation of these policies involves a meticulous process that requires input from various stakeholders and alignment with the organization's strategic objectives.

To initiate the development of governance policies, it is essential to conduct a comprehensive needs assessment. This assessment identifies the specific requirements and challenges faced by the organization in managing projects. Key areas of focus include project selection criteria, resource allocation, risk management, quality assurance, and performance measurement. The assessment should involve consultations with senior management, project managers, and other relevant stakeholders to gather diverse perspectives and insights.

Once the needs assessment is complete, the next step involves the formulation of a governance framework. This framework serves as the foundation for all subsequent policies and procedures. It typically includes the definition of the PMO's mission, vision, and objectives, as well as the establishment of guiding principles that reflect the organization's values and strategic priorities. The governance framework should also outline the PMO's organizational structure, including the roles and responsibilities of key personnel.

With the governance framework in place, the development of specific policies can commence. These policies should address critical aspects of project management, such as project initiation, planning, execution, monitoring, and closure. Each policy should be clearly articulated, detailing the processes, standards, and guidelines that must be followed. For example, a project initiation policy may outline the criteria for project approval, the documentation required, and the approval process. Similarly, a risk management policy may specify the procedures for identifying, assessing, and mitigating project risks.

To ensure the effectiveness of governance policies, it is crucial to establish mechanisms for compliance and enforcement. This includes the creation of monitoring and reporting systems that track adherence to established policies and identify any deviations. Regular audits and reviews should be conducted to assess the effectiveness of the policies and to make necessary adjustments. Additionally, training and development programs should be implemented to ensure that all personnel involved in project management are well-versed in the governance policies and understand their importance.

Stakeholder engagement plays a pivotal role in the successful implementation of governance policies. It is essential to foster a culture of collaboration and transparency, where stakeholders are encouraged to provide feedback and contribute to the continuous improvement of the governance framework. Regular communication and consultation with stakeholders help to build trust and ensure that the policies remain relevant and effective in addressing the evolving needs of the organization.

In conclusion, the establishment of governance policies is a foundational element in creating an effective PMO. It requires a systematic approach that includes a thorough needs assessment, the development of a governance framework, the formulation of specific policies, and the implementation of compliance mechanisms. By engaging stakeholders and fostering a culture of collaboration, organizations can ensure that their governance policies effectively support the PMO's mission and contribute to the successful management of projects.

Compliance and Standards

In the establishment of a Project Management Office (PMO), adherence to compliance and standards is crucial for ensuring operational efficiency and regulatory alignment. Compliance refers to the process of conforming to established guidelines, specifications, and legislations, which are often mandated by external bodies or internal governance frameworks. Standards, on the other hand, are set benchmarks or criteria that define the quality and consistency of processes and deliverables within the PMO.

To initiate compliance, it is essential to identify the relevant regulatory requirements that pertain to the organization's industry. This includes understanding local, national, and international laws, as well as industry-specific regulations. For instance, a PMO operating in the healthcare sector must comply with HIPAA (Health Insurance Portability and Accountability Act) regulations, while one in the financial sector must adhere to SOX (Sarbanes-Oxley Act) requirements. The identification process involves thorough research, consultation with legal experts, and continuous monitoring of regulatory updates.

Once the regulatory landscape is mapped out, the next step is to integrate these requirements into the PMO's processes. This can be achieved through the development of compliance checklists, standard operating procedures (SOPs), and regular training programs for the PMO staff. Compliance checklists serve as a tool to ensure that all necessary steps are taken to meet regulatory requirements, while SOPs provide detailed instructions on how to perform tasks in accordance with these regulations. Training programs are essential for keeping the staff updated on compliance policies and practices, thereby fostering a culture of compliance within the organization.

In parallel with compliance, the establishment of standards is necessary for maintaining consistency and quality in project management practices. Standards such as those set by the Project Management Institute (PMI) or the International Organization for Standardization (ISO) provide a framework for best practices in project management. For example, PMI's PMBOK (Project Management Body of Knowledge) offers guidelines on project integration, scope, time, cost, quality, human resources, communications, risk, and procurement management. Similarly, ISO 21500 provides guidance on project management concepts and processes.

The implementation of these standards involves several steps. First, the PMO needs to conduct a gap analysis to compare current practices with the desired standards. This analysis helps in identifying areas that require improvement. Following the gap analysis, a detailed plan should be developed to address the discrepancies. This plan may include revising existing processes, adopting new tools and technologies, and providing training to staff to align their skills with the standards.

Moreover, continuous monitoring and evaluation are vital to ensure ongoing compliance and adherence to standards. This can be facilitated through regular audits, performance reviews, and feedback mechanisms. Audits help in identifying non-compliance issues and areas where standards are not being met, allowing for timely corrective actions. Performance reviews and feedback from project teams provide insights into the effectiveness of the implemented standards and highlight opportunities for further improvement.

The integration of compliance and standards into the PMO not only ensures regulatory alignment but also enhances the overall quality and efficiency of project management practices. It fosters a structured approach to managing projects, reduces risks associated with non-compliance, and builds stakeholder confidence in the PMO's capability to deliver successful project outcomes.

Audit and Review

The establishment and maintenance of an effective Project Management Office (PMO) necessitate a rigorous approach to auditing and reviewing its processes, performance, and outcomes. This ensures that the PMO remains aligned with organizational goals, maintains high standards of project execution, and continuously improves its methodologies and practices.

A systematic audit process involves a comprehensive assessment of the PMO's adherence to its defined processes and procedures. This includes evaluating whether the PMO is following its own guidelines for project initiation, planning, execution, monitoring, and closure. Audits should be conducted regularly and should cover all aspects of the PMO's operations, including resource allocation, risk management, communication strategies, and stakeholder engagement. The audit team should comprise individuals with expertise in project management and audit practices, and they should operate with a clear mandate to identify any deviations from established protocols.

Reviewing the performance of the PMO involves analyzing key performance indicators (KPIs) and other metrics that reflect the efficiency and effectiveness of the PMO. Metrics such as project success rates, budget adherence, time-to-completion, and stakeholder satisfaction provide valuable insights into the PMO's performance. These metrics should be tracked over time to identify trends and areas for improvement. Regular performance reviews should be conducted, and the results should be communicated to senior management and other stakeholders to ensure transparency and accountability.

The audit and review process should also include a qualitative assessment of the PMO's impact on the organization. This involves gathering feedback from project managers, team members, and other stakeholders to understand their perspectives on the PMO's support and effectiveness. Surveys, interviews, and focus groups can be useful tools for collecting this feedback. The qualitative data should be analyzed alongside quantitative metrics to provide a holistic view of the PMO's performance.

Continuous improvement is a key objective of the audit and review process. Based on the findings from audits and performance reviews, the PMO should develop and implement action plans to address any identified issues or areas for improvement. This may involve revising processes, enhancing training programs, adopting new tools and technologies, or making organizational changes. The PMO should also establish mechanisms for tracking the implementation and effectiveness of these improvements.

It is crucial that the audit and review process is perceived as a constructive and collaborative effort rather than a punitive measure. The goal is to enhance the PMO's capabilities and ensure that it delivers maximum value to the organization. Therefore, the process should be conducted with a focus on learning and development, and the findings should be used to foster a culture of continuous improvement within the PMO.

The audit and review process should be an integral part of the PMO's governance framework. It should be supported by clear policies and procedures, and there should be a commitment from senior management to act on the findings. By systematically auditing and reviewing its operations, the PMO can ensure that it remains effective, efficient, and aligned with the strategic objectives of the organization.

Risk Management Policies

Effective risk management is a critical component of any Project Management Office (PMO) aiming to ensure project success and organizational resilience. A well-defined risk management policy provides a structured approach to identifying, assessing, and mitigating risks throughout the project lifecycle. This subchapter delineates the essential elements and best practices for developing robust risk management policies within a PMO framework.

The initial step in formulating a risk management policy involves the establishment of a risk management plan. This plan should outline the objectives, scope, and methodologies for risk management activities. It is imperative to define roles and responsibilities, ensuring that all stakeholders understand their contributions to risk identification and mitigation. The plan should also specify the criteria for risk prioritization, which typically considers both the likelihood of occurrence and the potential impact on project outcomes.

Risk identification is a continuous process that necessitates input from various project stakeholders. Techniques such as brainstorming sessions, expert interviews, and risk checklists can be employed to uncover potential risks. Additionally, historical data from past projects can provide valuable insights into recurring risks and their mitigation strategies. It is essential to document identified risks in a risk register, which serves as a centralized repository for tracking and managing risks.

Once risks are identified, they must be analyzed to determine their probability and impact. Quantitative risk analysis methods, such as Monte Carlo simulations or decision tree analysis, can provide a more precise assessment of risks. Conversely, qualitative methods, like risk probability and impact matrices, offer a simpler, yet effective, means of categorizing risks based on their severity. The outcome of this analysis should guide the prioritization of risks, enabling the PMO to focus its efforts on the most critical threats to project success.

Risk mitigation strategies are developed based on the prioritized risks. These strategies may include risk avoidance, where actions are taken to eliminate the risk; risk reduction, where measures are implemented to decrease the probability or impact of the risk; risk transfer, where the risk is shifted to a third party; and risk acceptance, where the risk is acknowledged, and contingency plans are established. It is crucial to assign risk owners who are responsible for implementing and monitoring these mitigation strategies. Regular reviews and updates to the risk register ensure that the PMO remains vigilant and responsive to emerging risks.

Communication is pivotal in the risk management process. The PMO should establish clear channels for reporting and discussing risks. Regular risk review meetings, involving key stakeholders, facilitate the exchange of information and the collective evaluation of risk mitigation efforts. Transparent communication fosters a culture of risk awareness and proactive management, thereby enhancing the overall effectiveness of the PMO.

Monitoring and controlling risks is an ongoing activity that requires diligent oversight. Key performance indicators (KPIs) and risk metrics should be established to measure the effectiveness of risk management activities. These metrics provide early warning signals and enable timely corrective actions. Additionally, lessons learned from risk management activities should be documented and integrated into the PMO's knowledge base, contributing to continuous improvement.

A comprehensive risk management policy not only safeguards project objectives but also aligns with the organization's strategic goals. By embedding risk management into the PMO's processes, organizations can navigate uncertainties with greater confidence and achieve sustainable project success. The development and implementation of such policies necessitate a commitment to continuous learning and adaptation, ensuring that the PMO remains resilient in the face of evolving project landscapes.

Continuous Improvement

Continuous improvement is a critical component in the establishment and maintenance of an effective Project Management Office (PMO). It involves the systematic and ongoing effort to enhance processes, services, and practices within the PMO framework. This subchapter delves into the methodologies, strategies, and tools that can be employed to foster a culture of continuous improvement within a PMO.

At its core, continuous improvement is anchored in the principles of Lean and Six Sigma, which advocate for the elimination of waste and reduction of variability in processes. These methodologies encourage an iterative approach to problem-solving, utilizing data-driven decision-making to identify and rectify inefficiencies. By embedding these principles, a PMO can achieve higher levels of efficiency, quality, and stakeholder satisfaction.

The first step in fostering continuous improvement is establishing a baseline through comprehensive process mapping. This involves documenting current processes in detail, identifying key performance indicators (KPIs), and assessing existing workflows. Process mapping provides a clear understanding of the current state, enabling the identification of bottlenecks, redundancies, and areas for enhancement. Tools such as flowcharts, swimlane diagrams, and value stream mapping are instrumental in this phase.

Once the baseline is established, the next phase involves the systematic collection and analysis of data. Quantitative data, such as cycle times, defect rates, and resource utilization, provide objective insights into process performance. Qualitative data, gathered through stakeholder feedback and observations, offer contextual understanding and highlight areas that may not be evident through quantitative analysis alone. Techniques such as root cause analysis, Pareto charts, and control charts are utilized to interpret the data, identify trends, and prioritize improvement initiatives.

A critical aspect of continuous improvement is the involvement of all stakeholders. Engaging team members, project managers, and stakeholders in the improvement process fosters a sense of ownership and accountability. Regular workshops, brainstorming sessions, and feedback loops are effective mechanisms for facilitating engagement and collaboration. The use of cross-functional teams ensures diverse perspectives are considered, leading to more robust and innovative solutions.

Implementation of improvement initiatives follows a structured approach, often guided by the Plan-Do-Check-Act (PDCA) cycle. In the planning phase, specific improvement goals are defined, and detailed action plans are developed. The execution phase involves piloting the proposed changes on a small scale to validate their effectiveness. The checking phase entails monitoring the outcomes using predefined metrics to assess the impact of the changes. Based on the results, adjustments are made, and successful improvements are standardized and scaled across the PMO.

Sustaining continuous improvement requires a supportive organizational culture. Leadership commitment is paramount, as it sets the tone for the importance of improvement efforts.

Leaders must actively promote and participate in continuous improvement activities, providing the necessary resources and support. Training and development programs are essential for equipping team members with the skills and knowledge required to contribute effectively to improvement initiatives.

Moreover, the integration of technology can significantly enhance continuous improvement efforts. Project management software, data analytics tools, and automation technologies streamline data collection, analysis, and reporting processes. These tools enable real-time monitoring of performance metrics, facilitating timely identification and resolution of issues.

Continuous improvement is not a one-time effort but an ongoing commitment to excellence. By embedding a culture of continuous improvement, a PMO can adapt to changing environments, meet evolving stakeholder needs, and achieve sustainable success. Through disciplined application of improvement methodologies, active stakeholder engagement, and leveraging technology, a PMO can continuously enhance its processes and deliver greater value.

Chapter 10: Performance Measurement and Reporting

Key Performance Indicators (KPIs)

Key Performance Indicators (KPIs) are integral to the successful operation of a Project Management Office (PMO). They serve as quantifiable metrics that allow organizations to evaluate the efficiency, effectiveness, and overall performance of their project management practices. Establishing KPIs is not merely a procedural task but a strategic endeavor that aligns the objectives of the PMO with the broader organizational goals.

The primary function of KPIs is to provide a clear, objective means of measuring progress against established benchmarks. These metrics facilitate the identification of areas needing improvement, the recognition of successful strategies, and the optimal allocation of resources. The selection of appropriate KPIs is critical, as these indicators must be relevant, actionable, and aligned with the strategic priorities of the organization.

A robust PMO typically employs a variety of KPIs to monitor different aspects of project management. Common categories include project performance, resource utilization, financial metrics, and stakeholder satisfaction. Project performance KPIs might encompass metrics such as project completion rates, adherence to timelines, and quality of deliverables. These indicators provide insights into the efficiency of project execution and the effectiveness of project planning processes.

Resource utilization KPIs focus on the optimal use of human, technological, and material resources. Metrics such as resource allocation efficiency, workload balance, and capacity utilization are critical for ensuring that resources are deployed effectively and that team members are neither overburdened nor underutilized. This category of KPIs helps in identifying bottlenecks and optimizing the distribution of resources across various projects.

Financial KPIs are essential for monitoring the economic aspects of project management. These metrics include budget adherence, cost variance, return on investment (ROI), and cost performance index (CPI). Financial KPIs enable the PMO to track expenditure, manage financial risks, and ensure that projects are delivered within budgetary constraints. They also aid in demonstrating the economic value generated by the PMO to organizational stakeholders.

Stakeholder satisfaction KPIs gauge the perceptions and satisfaction levels of various stakeholders, including clients, team members, and executive leadership. Metrics in this category might include stakeholder engagement levels, satisfaction surveys, and feedback scores. These indicators are crucial in maintaining positive stakeholder relationships and ensuring that project outcomes meet or exceed expectations.

The process of defining and implementing KPIs involves several key steps. Initially, it is essential to identify the strategic objectives of the PMO and the organization. This alignment ensures that the selected KPIs are relevant and supportive of broader goals. Subsequently, specific, measurable, achievable, relevant, and time-bound (SMART) criteria should be applied to each KPI to ensure clarity and focus.

Data collection and analysis are vital components of KPI management. Reliable and consistent data sources must be established to ensure the accuracy of KPI measurements. Advanced analytical tools and techniques can be employed to interpret the data, identify trends, and generate actionable insights. Regular reporting and review of KPIs are necessary to monitor progress, make informed decisions, and drive continuous improvement.

Effective communication of KPI results is equally important. Transparent reporting mechanisms should be in place to share KPI findings with relevant stakeholders. Visual aids such as dashboards and scorecards can enhance the understanding and impact of KPI data. Engaging stakeholders in discussions about KPI outcomes fosters a culture of accountability and continuous improvement within the PMO.

In conclusion, KPIs are a cornerstone of effective PMO management. They provide a structured approach to monitoring and enhancing project performance, resource utilization, financial management, and stakeholder satisfaction. By carefully selecting, implementing, and communicating KPIs, a PMO can significantly contribute to the achievement of organizational objectives and the realization of strategic goals.

Data Collection Methods

Effective data collection is paramount in establishing a Project Management Office (PMO) that can drive organizational success. Various methodologies can be employed to gather accurate and relevant data, each with its own set of advantages and challenges. Understanding these methods enables PMO leaders to make informed decisions, optimize processes, and enhance project outcomes.

Surveys and questionnaires are among the most common data collection tools. They offer a structured way to gather quantitative data from a broad audience. Surveys can be distributed electronically, making them cost-effective and easy to administer. Designing effective surveys involves crafting clear, concise questions that minimize bias and elicit meaningful responses. Closed-ended questions provide quantifiable data, while open-ended questions can offer deeper insights into respondents' perspectives. The data collected through surveys can be analyzed statistically to identify trends, patterns, and areas for improvement.

Interviews provide a qualitative approach to data collection, allowing for a deeper exploration of specific issues. Conducting one-on-one or group interviews with key stakeholders, project managers, and team members can reveal nuanced information that might not surface through surveys. Interviews can be structured, semi-structured, or unstructured, depending on the level of flexibility required. Structured interviews follow a predefined set of questions, ensuring consistency across interviews. Semi-structured interviews allow for some flexibility, enabling the interviewer to probe further based on the responses. Unstructured interviews are more conversational, providing the opportunity to explore topics in depth. Recording and transcribing interviews facilitate a thorough analysis of the qualitative data.

Focus groups are another qualitative method that involves a facilitated discussion among a diverse group of participants. This approach can generate rich, detailed data through the interaction and exchange of ideas. Focus groups are particularly useful for exploring complex issues, generating new ideas, and understanding the collective views of different stakeholders. The facilitator plays a crucial role in guiding the discussion, ensuring that all participants have the opportunity to contribute. Analyzing focus group data involves identifying common themes, patterns, and divergences in participants' responses.

Observations allow for the collection of real-time data by directly witnessing processes and behaviors. This method can be particularly useful for understanding the actual workflow, identifying bottlenecks, and verifying the accuracy of reported data. Observations can be participant-based, where the observer becomes part of the activity, or non-participant, where the observer remains detached. Detailed field notes and video recordings can enhance the accuracy and reliability of observational data. Analyzing observational data involves coding and categorizing behaviors, processes, and interactions to identify key issues and opportunities for improvement.

Document analysis involves reviewing existing documentation, such as project reports, meeting minutes, and performance metrics. This method provides historical and contextual data that can help in understanding past performance and identifying trends. Document analysis is non-intrusive and can be conducted without disrupting ongoing activities. However, the quality and completeness of the documents can impact the reliability of the data. Triangulating document analysis with other data collection methods can enhance the robustness of the findings.

Combining multiple data collection methods, known as triangulation, can provide a more comprehensive and reliable understanding of the PMO's performance and challenges. Triangulation helps to validate findings by cross-verifying data from different sources. Each method has its inherent strengths and limitations, and using a mix of methods can mitigate the weaknesses of individual approaches.

Selecting the appropriate data collection methods depends on the specific objectives, resources, and context of the PMO. A well-planned data collection strategy ensures that the gathered data is accurate, relevant, and actionable, forming the foundation for effective decision-making and continuous improvement within the PMO.

Dashboard and Reporting Tools

A pivotal element in the establishment of an effective Project Management Office (PMO) is the implementation of robust dashboard and reporting tools. These tools serve as the backbone for data-driven decision-making processes, enabling project managers and stakeholders to monitor project progress, identify potential risks, and ensure alignment with organizational goals.

Dashboards act as a visual representation of key performance indicators (KPIs) and other critical metrics. They consolidate data from various sources into an intuitive and interactive interface, providing real-time insights into project health and performance. The design of an effective dashboard should prioritize clarity, relevance, and usability. Key metrics such as project timelines, budget adherence, resource allocation, and risk status should be prominently displayed. Customizability is also essential, allowing users to tailor the dashboard to their specific needs and preferences.

The selection of appropriate dashboard tools requires careful consideration of several factors. These include integration capabilities with existing systems, user-friendliness, scalability, and the ability to support multiple data sources. Advanced features like drill-down capabilities, predictive analytics, and automated alerts can significantly enhance the utility of dashboards. For instance, drill-down features enable users to explore underlying data layers for a more granular analysis, while predictive analytics can forecast potential project outcomes based on historical data trends.

Reporting tools complement dashboards by providing detailed, structured, and often narrative insights into project performance. These reports can be generated at various intervals—daily, weekly, monthly, or project-specific milestones—depending on the needs of the PMO and its stakeholders. Effective reporting tools should facilitate the creation of comprehensive reports that include quantitative data, qualitative analysis, and actionable recommendations. Integration with other PMO tools and systems is crucial to ensure that reports are generated based on accurate and up-to-date information.

Automation plays a critical role in enhancing the efficiency and accuracy of reporting processes. Automated reporting tools can streamline the collection, analysis, and dissemination of data, reducing the manual effort required and minimizing the risk of human error. These tools can also support the generation of customized reports tailored to different audiences, such as senior management, project teams, or external stakeholders.

The implementation of dashboard and reporting tools should be accompanied by a well-defined governance framework. This framework should outline the roles and responsibilities of individuals involved in data management, the protocols for data collection and validation, and the procedures for report generation and distribution. Training programs should be established to ensure that all users are proficient in utilizing the tools and interpreting the data presented.

It is also important to establish feedback mechanisms to continuously improve the effectiveness of dashboards and reporting tools. Regular reviews and updates based on user feedback and evolving project requirements can help to ensure that these tools remain relevant and valuable. Additionally, leveraging industry best practices and benchmarking against other PMOs can provide insights into potential areas for enhancement.

The integration of dashboard and reporting tools within a PMO not only facilitates effective project management but also promotes a culture of transparency and accountability. By providing a clear and comprehensive view of project performance, these tools enable informed decision-making, timely interventions, and the continuous improvement of project management processes.

Analyzing Performance Data

Performance data forms the cornerstone for evaluating the effectiveness of a Project Management Office (PMO). The process of analyzing this data involves a structured approach to ensure that insights derived are accurate, actionable, and aligned with organizational objectives. This subchapter delves into the methodologies and tools essential for scrutinizing performance data within a PMO context.

Initially, the collection of performance data must be systematic and comprehensive. Key performance indicators (KPIs) should be predefined, reflecting both the strategic goals of the organization and the operational metrics pertinent to project management. Typical KPIs include project completion rates, budget adherence, resource utilization, and stakeholder satisfaction. These metrics provide a quantitative basis for analysis and facilitate comparisons over time or across different projects.

Once data collection mechanisms are in place, the next step involves data preprocessing. This phase includes data cleaning to remove inconsistencies, handling missing values, and ensuring data integrity. Statistical techniques such as outlier detection and normalization are often employed to prepare the data for subsequent analysis. The use of software tools like Excel, R, or Python can streamline these preprocessing tasks, allowing for more accurate and efficient handling of large datasets.

With clean and reliable data, the analysis can proceed through various statistical and analytical techniques. Descriptive statistics provide a summary of the data, offering insights into central tendencies, variances, and distributions. These summaries help in understanding the general performance trends and identifying any anomalies or patterns that warrant further investigation.

Inferential statistics extend the analysis by enabling predictions and generalizations about the population from which the data sample is drawn. Techniques such as regression analysis, hypothesis testing, and confidence intervals can be applied to understand relationships between different variables and to test the significance of observed patterns. For instance, regression analysis might reveal how project duration impacts budget adherence, offering valuable insights for future project planning.

Advanced analytical methods, such as multivariate analysis and machine learning algorithms, can further enhance the depth of the analysis. These methods allow for the exploration of complex relationships and the identification of hidden patterns within the data. Clustering algorithms, for example, can segment projects into different categories based on performance metrics, enabling tailored strategies for improvement.

Visualization tools play a crucial role in making the analysis comprehensible and actionable. Dashboards and visual reports can transform raw data into intuitive graphs and charts, highlighting key insights and trends. Tools such as Tableau,

Power BI, and D3.js are instrumental in creating dynamic and interactive visualizations that facilitate better decision-making.

Interpreting the results of the analysis is perhaps the most critical step. It involves contextualizing the findings within the broader organizational framework and translating data insights into actionable strategies. This requires collaboration between data analysts, project managers, and senior leadership to ensure that the interpretations align with strategic goals and operational realities.

Continuous monitoring and iterative analysis are vital for maintaining the relevance and accuracy of performance data. Regular updates to the data collection mechanisms, KPIs, and analytical models ensure that the PMO remains responsive to changing project environments and organizational priorities. Feedback loops, where insights from the analysis inform subsequent data collection and analysis cycles, enhance the adaptability and effectiveness of the PMO.

In essence, the rigorous analysis of performance data empowers a PMO to make informed decisions, optimize project outcomes, and drive continuous improvement. By leveraging statistical and analytical techniques, visualization tools, and collaborative interpretation, a PMO can transform raw data into strategic insights, ultimately enhancing its contribution to organizational success.

Reporting to Stakeholders

Effective communication with stakeholders is a critical component of a successfully functioning Project Management Office (PMO). The establishment of a reporting mechanism ensures that stakeholders are kept informed of project progress, risks, issues, and performance metrics, fostering transparency and trust. The choice of reporting tools and techniques should be aligned with the stakeholders' needs and expectations to facilitate informed decision-making.

A structured reporting framework is essential to deliver consistent and accurate information. This framework should include regular updates on project status, budget adherence, timeline progress, and key performance indicators (KPIs). The frequency and format of these reports should be tailored to the preferences of different stakeholder groups. For instance, executive stakeholders may prefer high-level summaries, while project teams may require detailed reports.

The implementation of dashboards is an effective method for real-time reporting. Dashboards provide a visual representation of project data, allowing stakeholders to quickly grasp the current status and identify any areas requiring attention. These dashboards should be customizable to display relevant metrics and should be accessible through various devices to accommodate stakeholders' needs.

Risk reporting is another crucial aspect of stakeholder communication. Identifying, assessing, and communicating risks in a timely manner can prevent potential issues from escalating. A risk register, regularly updated and shared with stakeholders, ensures that all parties are aware of potential threats and the mitigation strategies in place. Including a risk heat map in reports can visually highlight the severity and likelihood of risks, aiding stakeholders in prioritizing their focus.

Issue tracking and reporting are equally important. A systematic approach to documenting issues, their impact, and the actions taken to resolve them provides stakeholders with assurance that the project is being managed effectively. Regular updates on issue resolution progress should be included in status reports to maintain transparency.

Budget reporting should detail actual expenditures against planned budgets, highlighting any variances and their causes. This information is vital for stakeholders to understand the financial health of the project and to make decisions regarding resource allocation. Forecasting future budget needs based on current trends can also help stakeholders anticipate and plan for potential financial requirements.

Timeline reporting should include updates on project milestones, deliverables, and any deviations from the planned schedule. Gantt charts and project timelines can be useful tools to visually communicate progress and identify any delays. Providing explanations for any deviations and outlining corrective actions helps stakeholders understand the project's trajectory and the measures being taken to stay on track.

Performance metrics should be clearly defined and reported regularly. These metrics might include project completion rates, quality measures, resource utilization, and customer satisfaction levels. Consistent tracking and reporting of these metrics enable stakeholders to gauge the project's success and identify areas for improvement.

Effective stakeholder reporting also involves regular meetings and presentations. These interactions provide an opportunity for stakeholders to ask questions, provide feedback, and engage in discussions about the project's direction. Meeting minutes and action items should be documented and shared to ensure accountability and follow-through.

In summary, the establishment of a robust reporting mechanism is paramount for the success of a PMO. By delivering accurate, timely, and relevant information, the PMO can foster a collaborative environment where stakeholders are well-informed and actively engaged in the project's progress. This transparency not only builds trust but also enhances the decision-making process, ultimately contributing to the project's overall success.

Chapter 11: Scaling the PMO

Assessing Readiness for Scaling

Evaluating an organization's preparedness for scaling a Project Management Office (PMO) is a critical step in ensuring the successful expansion and integration of project management practices across the enterprise. This evaluation requires a thorough analysis of current processes, resources, and organizational culture to identify potential gaps and areas for improvement. Establishing a comprehensive framework to assess readiness involves examining several key dimensions, including organizational alignment, resource availability, process maturity, and stakeholder engagement.

Organizational alignment refers to the degree to which the PMO's objectives and strategies are in harmony with the broader goals and priorities of the organization. It is essential to ensure that the PMO's vision is clearly articulated and understood by all relevant stakeholders. This includes aligning the PMO's initiatives with the strategic objectives of the organization, thereby ensuring that the PMO contributes to the overall success of the enterprise. A misalignment can lead to conflicts, reduced support, and suboptimal utilization of the PMO's capabilities.

Resource availability encompasses both human and technical resources. A successful scaling of the PMO necessitates a careful assessment of the current workforce, including their skills, experience, and capacity to take on additional responsibilities. It is imperative to identify any skill gaps and provide necessary training and development programs to equip the team with the required competencies. Additionally, evaluating the availability and adequacy of technological tools and infrastructure is crucial. This includes project management software, communication platforms, and data analytics tools that support the efficient execution and monitoring of projects.

Process maturity is another critical dimension that determines an organization's readiness for scaling its PMO. This involves evaluating the current state of project management processes, methodologies, and frameworks in use. A mature process environment is characterized by well-defined, standardized, and repeatable processes that are consistently followed across projects. Conducting a maturity assessment, such as utilizing models like the Capability Maturity Model Integration (CMMI), can provide valuable insights into areas that require enhancement. Organizations with higher process maturity levels are better positioned to scale their PMO effectively, as they can leverage established best practices and lessons learned.

Stakeholder engagement plays a pivotal role in the successful scaling of a PMO. It is vital to identify and engage key stakeholders, including executive sponsors, project managers, team members, and end-users, to garner their support and commitment. Effective communication strategies should be employed to keep stakeholders informed and involved throughout the scaling process. This includes regular updates on progress, addressing concerns, and incorporating feedback to ensure that the PMO's initiatives are aligned with stakeholder expectations and needs.

Conducting a readiness assessment involves utilizing various tools and techniques to gather data and insights. Surveys, interviews, workshops, and document reviews are commonly used methods to collect information from different parts of the organization. Analyzing this data helps in identifying strengths, weaknesses, opportunities, and threats related to scaling the PMO. The insights gained from this assessment form the basis for developing a tailored action plan that addresses identified gaps and leverages existing strengths.

A systematic and methodical approach to assessing readiness for scaling a PMO ensures that the organization is well-prepared to undertake this transformative initiative. By focusing on organizational alignment, resource availability, process maturity, and stakeholder engagement, organizations can create a solid foundation for the successful expansion of their project management capabilities. This preparatory phase is crucial in mitigating risks, optimizing resource utilization, and achieving the desired outcomes from the scaled PMO.

Scaling Strategies

Effective scaling of a Project Management Office (PMO) is critical to ensuring its sustainability and ability to meet the evolving needs of an organization. The process of scaling a PMO involves a series of strategic decisions and actions that align with the organization's growth trajectory and complexity of its project portfolio. This subchapter delineates the core strategies to effectively scale a PMO, focusing on structural adjustments, process optimizations, and technological advancements.

A primary consideration in scaling a PMO is the structural realignment to accommodate increased project demands. Initially, small PMOs may operate with a limited number of project managers and support staff. As the volume and complexity of projects grow, it becomes essential to expand the team. This expansion often necessitates the introduction of specialized roles, such as portfolio managers, program managers, and PMO analysts. These roles help distribute responsibilities more effectively, ensuring that each aspect of project management receives the necessary attention and expertise. Additionally, establishing a clear hierarchical structure with defined roles and responsibilities is crucial for maintaining efficiency and accountability.

Another key aspect of scaling a PMO is the optimization of processes and methodologies. Standardizing project management practices across the organization provides a consistent framework that enhances coordination and reduces ambiguities. Implementing robust governance frameworks ensures that projects are aligned with organizational goals and are delivered within scope, time, and budget constraints. Furthermore, adopting agile methodologies can offer flexibility and adaptability, which are essential for handling an increasing number of diverse projects. Continuous process improvement, through regular reviews and feedback loops, ensures that the PMO remains responsive to the dynamic business environment.

Technological advancements play a pivotal role in the scaling process. Investing in advanced project management software and tools can significantly enhance the efficiency and effectiveness of a PMO. These tools facilitate better resource management, real-time tracking, and comprehensive reporting, which are vital for managing larger project portfolios. Automation of routine tasks, such as scheduling, reporting, and monitoring, frees up valuable time for project managers to focus on strategic activities. Additionally, leveraging data analytics provides insights into project performance and helps in making informed decisions, thereby improving overall project outcomes.

The cultural aspect of scaling a PMO cannot be overlooked. As the PMO grows, fostering a culture of collaboration and continuous learning becomes increasingly important. Encouraging knowledge sharing and best practices across the team promotes a cohesive and supportive environment. Providing ongoing training and development opportunities ensures that the team is equipped with the latest skills and knowledge to handle complex projects. Recognizing and rewarding achievements also plays a crucial role in maintaining high morale and motivation among team members.

Stakeholder engagement is another critical component in the scaling strategy. Effective communication with stakeholders at all levels ensures that their expectations are managed and that they remain supportive of the PMO's initiatives. Regular updates and transparent reporting build trust and credibility, which are essential for securing the necessary resources and support for continued growth.

In conclusion, scaling a PMO involves a multifaceted approach that encompasses structural realignment, process optimization, technological enhancements, cultural development, and stakeholder engagement. By strategically addressing these areas, organizations can build a robust and adaptable PMO that is capable of supporting their long-term objectives and delivering sustained value.

Maintaining Quality

A robust Project Management Office (PMO) is instrumental in ensuring the consistent delivery of high-quality projects. To maintain quality, it is imperative to establish standardized processes and rigorous quality control mechanisms. This chapter delves into the methodologies and best practices essential for sustaining quality in a PMO.

Central to maintaining quality is the development and implementation of standardized project management processes. These processes should be meticulously documented and communicated to all stakeholders. Standardization minimizes variability and ensures that all team members adhere to the same protocols, thereby enhancing consistency across projects. A comprehensive process documentation should include detailed guidelines on project initiation, planning, execution, monitoring, and closure. Regular training sessions and workshops can be organized to familiarize the team with these processes and encourage adherence.

Quality control mechanisms are equally critical. These mechanisms involve continuous monitoring and evaluation of project activities to ensure they align with the predefined quality standards. Implementing a robust quality assurance (QA) framework is essential. The QA framework should encompass a variety of techniques, including peer reviews, audits, and testing protocols. Peer reviews can be conducted at various stages of the project to identify and rectify potential issues early. Audits, both internal and external, provide an objective assessment of the project's adherence to quality standards. Testing protocols, particularly in software development projects, are vital to ensure that the final deliverables meet the required specifications.

The role of metrics and Key Performance Indicators (KPIs) in maintaining quality cannot be overstated. Metrics provide quantifiable data that can be analyzed to gauge the performance and quality of projects. KPIs should be carefully selected to reflect the critical aspects of project quality. Common KPIs include defect density, customer satisfaction, and adherence to timelines and budgets. Regularly tracking these KPIs enables the PMO to identify trends, pinpoint areas needing improvement, and implement corrective actions promptly.

Stakeholder engagement is another crucial element in maintaining quality. Effective communication with stakeholders ensures that their expectations and requirements are clearly understood and met. Regular status updates, review meetings, and feedback sessions facilitate a transparent and collaborative environment. This engagement helps in aligning the project outcomes with stakeholder expectations, thereby enhancing the perceived quality of the project.

Continuous improvement is a cornerstone of quality maintenance. The PMO should foster a culture of continuous improvement by encouraging feedback and learning from past projects. Post-project reviews and retrospectives are valuable tools in this regard. These reviews should be conducted systematically to analyze the successes and challenges faced during the project. The insights gained from these reviews can be used to refine processes, update documentation, and implement best practices in future projects.

Investing in technology and tools can significantly aid in maintaining quality. Project management software, quality management systems, and collaboration tools enhance efficiency and accuracy in project execution. These tools provide real-time data, facilitate seamless communication, and automate repetitive tasks, thereby reducing the margin for error and ensuring adherence to quality standards.

Maintaining quality in a PMO is a multifaceted endeavor that requires a strategic approach, involving standardized processes, rigorous quality control mechanisms, effective stakeholder engagement, continuous improvement, and the judicious use of technology. By integrating these elements, a PMO can consistently deliver high-quality projects that meet or exceed stakeholder expectations.

Managing Increased Complexity

As organizations scale and projects proliferate, the complexity inherent in project management endeavors increases substantially. Effective Project Management Offices (PMOs) play a pivotal role in navigating this complexity by implementing structured methodologies and robust governance frameworks. A PMO serves as the centralized entity that standardizes processes, enforces compliance, and provides the necessary support to ensure that projects align with organizational objectives and deliver value.

One of the primary challenges in managing increased complexity is maintaining consistency across multiple projects. This is achieved through the establishment of standardized templates and processes. Standardization not only reduces redundancy but also facilitates seamless communication and coordination among project teams. By employing a uniform set of guidelines, the PMO ensures that all projects adhere to best practices and organizational standards, thereby minimizing risks and enhancing efficiency.

Another critical aspect is resource management. As projects become more intricate, the demand for skilled resources escalates. The PMO must develop a comprehensive resource management strategy that includes resource allocation, capacity planning, and skill development. Advanced tools such as resource management software can be leveraged to track resource utilization, forecast demand, and identify skill gaps. By optimizing resource allocation, the PMO can ensure that the right resources are available at the right time, thus preventing bottlenecks and ensuring project continuity.

Risk management is also paramount in handling increased complexity. Complex projects are inherently fraught with uncertainties and potential pitfalls. The PMO must adopt a proactive approach to risk management by identifying potential risks early, assessing their impact, and devising mitigation strategies. This involves regular risk assessments, the establishment of risk registers, and the implementation of contingency plans. By systematically managing risks, the PMO can minimize disruptions and safeguard project outcomes.

Effective communication is indispensable in a complex project environment. The PMO must facilitate transparent and continuous communication among stakeholders, project teams, and management. This can be achieved through regular status meetings, progress reports, and collaborative platforms that enable real-time information sharing. Clear and consistent communication ensures that all parties are informed of project developments, potential issues, and decisions, thereby fostering a collaborative and cohesive project environment.

The integration of advanced technology is another critical factor in managing complexity. Modern PMOs must leverage digital tools such as project management software, data analytics, and automation to streamline processes and enhance decision-making. These tools provide real-time insights into project performance, enable data-driven decision-making, and automate routine tasks, thereby reducing manual effort and increasing efficiency. By harnessing technology, the PMO can better manage the intricacies of complex projects and deliver superior outcomes.

Moreover, the PMO must foster a culture of continuous improvement. This involves regularly reviewing and refining processes, incorporating feedback, and staying abreast of industry trends and best practices. Continuous improvement ensures that the PMO remains agile and responsive to changing project dynamics and organizational needs. By promoting a culture of learning and innovation, the PMO can enhance its capability to manage complexity and drive project success.

In essence, managing increased complexity requires a multifaceted approach that encompasses standardization, resource management, risk management, effective communication, technological integration, and continuous improvement. By adopting these strategies, the PMO can effectively navigate the challenges of complex project environments and deliver consistent, high-quality results.

Case Studies of Scaled PMOs

Various organizations have implemented Project Management Offices (PMOs) at scale with varying degrees of success. Examining these case studies provides valuable insights into the strategies, challenges, and outcomes associated with scaling PMOs. This subchapter delves into several real-world examples, highlighting the practices that led to effective PMO implementations and the lessons learned along the way.

One notable example is a large multinational corporation in the technology sector. This organization sought to standardize project management practices across its numerous global divisions. Initially, the PMO faced resistance due to the diverse project management methodologies already in use. To address this, the PMO conducted a thorough needs assessment and engaged with key stakeholders to define a unified framework. This framework incorporated elements from various methodologies, allowing for flexibility while ensuring consistency in reporting and performance metrics. By fostering a collaborative environment and providing extensive training, the PMO achieved buy-in from all divisions, resulting in improved project outcomes and streamlined processes.

In another case, a financial services company aimed to enhance its project portfolio management through a centralized PMO. The company struggled with aligning projects to strategic objectives and managing resources efficiently. The PMO introduced a robust portfolio management tool that provided real-time visibility into project statuses and resource allocations. Additionally, the PMO implemented governance structures to prioritize projects based on strategic value. This approach enabled the organization to make informed decisions, optimize resource utilization, and deliver projects that significantly contributed to business goals. The success of this PMO was attributed to its focus on strategic alignment and data-driven decision-making.

A healthcare provider faced challenges in managing large-scale IT projects critical to its operations. The PMO in this context adopted a phased implementation strategy, starting with a pilot program in one department. This pilot allowed the PMO to refine its processes and demonstrate value before scaling across the entire organization. The phased approach minimized disruptions and provided a blueprint for broader implementation. The PMO also emphasized continuous improvement, regularly reviewing and adjusting its methodologies based on feedback and performance data. This iterative process ensured that the PMO remained agile and responsive to the evolving needs of the organization.

An aerospace and defense company provides another illustrative case. This organization required stringent compliance with industry regulations and standards. The PMO developed comprehensive compliance checklists and integrated them into the project lifecycle. Regular audits and reviews ensured adherence to regulatory requirements, reducing the risk of non-compliance. The PMO also established a knowledge repository to capture best practices and lessons learned, facilitating continuous learning and improvement. By embedding compliance into the PMO's processes, the organization maintained high standards and mitigated risks effectively.

A public sector agency aimed to improve transparency and accountability in its project management practices. The PMO introduced standardized templates and reporting mechanisms, ensuring consistent documentation and communication across projects. Regular status meetings and progress reports enhanced visibility and stakeholder engagement. The PMO also focused on building a project management culture within the agency, offering training programs and certifications to develop project management competencies among staff. These initiatives led to increased project success rates and greater stakeholder confidence in the agency's project management capabilities.

These case studies underscore the importance of tailored approaches in scaling PMOs. Successful implementations often involve customizing methodologies to fit organizational contexts, prioritizing strategic alignment, fostering stakeholder engagement, and emphasizing continuous improvement. By learning from these examples, organizations can navigate the complexities of scaling PMOs and achieve their project management objectives more effectively.

Chapter 12: Risk Management in PMO

Identifying Risks

Effective project management is contingent upon the ability to foresee potential obstacles and mitigate them before they materialize. Identifying risks is a fundamental activity within the framework of a Project Management Office (PMO) that ensures project success. This process involves systematically uncovering, analyzing, and prioritizing potential threats that could impede project objectives.

The initial step in risk identification is to establish a comprehensive understanding of the project's scope, objectives, and constraints. This holistic view enables the identification of internal and external factors that may influence project performance. Internal factors include resource availability, team competency, and technological infrastructure, while external factors encompass market dynamics, regulatory changes, and stakeholder expectations.

A robust risk identification process employs various methodologies to ensure thoroughness. One widely-used approach is brainstorming sessions involving key project stakeholders. These sessions facilitate the collective identification of risks through diverse perspectives. Another method is the Delphi technique, which leverages the expertise of a panel of specialists through iterative rounds of anonymous feedback. This technique reduces the influence of dominant voices, ensuring an unbiased risk assessment.

Additionally, historical data analysis provides valuable insights into potential risks based on past project experiences. By examining lessons learned from previous projects, the PMO can identify recurring issues and anticipate similar challenges. This retrospective analysis is complemented by checklists and risk breakdown structures (RBS), which categorize risks into hierarchical frameworks for systematic examination.

A more structured approach involves the application of SWOT (Strengths, Weaknesses, Opportunities, Threats) analysis. This technique enables the identification of internal and external factors that can positively or negatively affect the project. Strengths and opportunities are leveraged to counteract weaknesses and threats, thereby enhancing the project's resilience.

Furthermore, the use of risk registers is pivotal in documenting identified risks. A risk register is a dynamic tool that captures detailed information about each risk, including its description, potential impact, likelihood of occurrence, and proposed mitigation strategies. This documentation facilitates continuous monitoring and updating of risks as the project progresses.

Engaging in stakeholder analysis is also crucial. Different stakeholders have varied interests and perceptions of risk, which can influence the project's risk profile. Identifying and understanding these perspectives allows for the anticipation of stakeholder-related risks and the development of targeted communication and mitigation plans.

Advanced techniques such as Failure Mode and Effects Analysis (FMEA) and Monte Carlo simulation offer quantitative approaches to risk identification. FMEA systematically evaluates potential failure points and their effects on the project, prioritizing them based on severity, occurrence, and detection likelihood. Monte Carlo simulation, on the other hand, uses probabilistic models to predict the impact of risks, providing a range of possible outcomes and their associated probabilities.

Incorporating risk identification into the early stages of project planning is essential for proactive risk management. This proactive stance enables the PMO to allocate resources effectively, devise contingency plans, and establish robust monitoring mechanisms. By systematically identifying and addressing risks, the PMO enhances the likelihood of project success and fosters a culture of continuous improvement.

The efficacy of risk identification hinges on the PMO's ability to adapt and refine its processes. As projects evolve, new risks emerge, necessitating ongoing vigilance and adaptability. A well-established risk identification process is not static but evolves with the project's lifecycle, ensuring that the PMO remains agile and responsive to emerging threats.

Risk Assessment Techniques

Effective risk assessment is a cornerstone of Project Management Office (PMO) success. Implementing robust risk assessment techniques enables a PMO to identify, evaluate, and mitigate potential risks that could impede project objectives. Various methodologies can be employed to assess risks, each offering unique insights and benefits.

Qualitative risk assessment is a widely used technique that involves the evaluation of risk based on its probability and impact. This approach utilizes tools such as risk matrices and heat maps to prioritize risks. The process begins with risk identification, often facilitated by brainstorming sessions, expert interviews, and workshops. Risks are then qualitatively evaluated to determine their severity, typically categorized as high, medium, or low. This method is advantageous for its simplicity and speed, allowing teams to quickly identify critical risks and allocate resources accordingly.

Quantitative risk assessment provides a more numerical approach to risk evaluation. Techniques such as Monte Carlo simulations, decision tree analysis, and sensitivity analysis are employed to quantify the potential impact of risks. Monte Carlo simulations, for instance, use probability distributions to simulate a range of possible outcomes, offering a probabilistic view of risk. Decision tree analysis helps in understanding the implications of various decisions in the presence of uncertainty. Sensitivity analysis identifies how changes in one or more input variables affect the overall risk profile. These quantitative methods are beneficial for their precision, enabling detailed risk modeling and informed decision-making.

Another effective technique is Failure Mode and Effects Analysis (FMEA), which systematically evaluates potential failure modes within a process and their effects on project outcomes. FMEA involves identifying failure modes, determining their causes and effects, and prioritizing them based on their severity, occurrence, and detectability. This method is particularly useful in engineering and manufacturing projects, where understanding the intricacies of potential failures is critical.

Risk workshops and facilitated sessions are interactive techniques that engage project stakeholders in the risk assessment process. These sessions often employ structured approaches such as the Delphi method, where experts provide independent risk assessments that are then aggregated to form a consensus. The collaborative nature of these workshops ensures diverse perspectives are considered, enhancing the comprehensiveness of the risk assessment.

Scenario analysis is another technique that explores different future scenarios and their potential impacts on project objectives. By developing and analyzing multiple scenarios, a PMO can better understand the range of possible risks and prepare contingency plans. This method is particularly valuable in projects with high uncertainty or those operating in volatile environments.

Swimlane diagrams, also known as cross-functional flowcharts, can be used to visualize processes and identify potential risk points. By mapping out the flow of activities and responsibilities, these diagrams help pinpoint areas where risks may arise due to handoffs or dependencies. This visual approach enhances understanding and communication among team members.

Each risk assessment technique offers distinct advantages and can be selected based on the specific needs and context of the project. A combination of qualitative and quantitative methods often yields the best results, providing a balanced view of both the likelihood and impact of risks. Adopting a systematic approach to risk assessment enables PMOs to proactively manage uncertainties, ensuring project objectives are met with minimal disruptions. Effective risk assessment is not a one-time activity but an ongoing process that requires continuous monitoring and adjustment to adapt to changing project dynamics.

Developing Risk Mitigation Plans

Risk mitigation planning is a critical component of effective Project Management Office (PMO) operations. It involves identifying potential risks, assessing their impact, and developing strategies to minimize their effects on project objectives. The systematic approach to risk mitigation ensures that projects are more likely to be completed on time, within budget, and to the desired quality standards.

The first step in developing risk mitigation plans is risk identification. This process involves a thorough analysis of the project environment to uncover potential risks. Techniques such as brainstorming sessions, expert interviews, and SWOT

(Strengths, Weaknesses, Opportunities, Threats) analysis are commonly employed. It is crucial to document all identified risks in a risk register, which serves as a central repository for risk information.

Once risks are identified, the next step is risk assessment. This involves evaluating the likelihood of each risk occurring and the potential impact on the project. Quantitative methods such as probability-impact matrices and qualitative methods like expert judgment are used to prioritize risks. Higher-priority risks require more immediate and robust mitigation strategies.

Developing mitigation strategies involves determining the best course of action to address identified risks. There are four primary risk response strategies: avoidance, transfer, mitigation, and acceptance. Avoidance involves changing project plans to eliminate the risk. Transfer shifts the risk to a third party, such as through insurance or outsourcing. Mitigation reduces the likelihood or impact of the risk, often through proactive measures. Acceptance involves acknowledging the risk and preparing contingency plans in case it occurs.

Each risk response strategy requires detailed planning and resource allocation. For instance, risk mitigation might involve additional training for team members, procurement of specialized equipment, or implementation of new processes.

These plans must be documented and integrated into the overall project management plan. It is also important to assign responsibility for each risk mitigation action to specific team members to ensure accountability.

Monitoring and controlling risks is an ongoing process throughout the project lifecycle. Regular risk reviews and updates to the risk register are necessary to keep track of new risks and changes to existing ones. Key performance indicators (KPIs) and risk metrics should be established to measure the effectiveness of risk mitigation efforts. Automated tools and software can assist in tracking and managing risks more efficiently.

Communication plays a vital role in risk mitigation planning. All stakeholders, including project team members, sponsors, and clients, must be kept informed about risks and mitigation plans. Regular status meetings and reports ensure that everyone is aware of current risks and the steps being taken to address them. Transparent communication fosters a culture of risk awareness and proactive management within the PMO.

Training and development are essential to enhance the risk management capabilities of the PMO team. Regular workshops, seminars, and training sessions on risk management methodologies and tools can improve the team's ability to identify, assess, and mitigate risks effectively. Investing in continuous learning ensures that the PMO stays current with best practices and emerging trends in risk management.

In conclusion, developing risk mitigation plans is a structured and systematic process that is integral to the success of any project managed by a PMO. By identifying, assessing, and addressing risks proactively, PMOs can enhance project outcomes and contribute to the overall stability and success of the organization.

Monitoring Risks

Effective risk management is a critical component of a successful Project Management Office (PMO). The process of monitoring risks involves the continuous identification, assessment, and tracking of potential issues that could impact project outcomes. This subchapter delves into the mechanisms and methodologies for maintaining vigilance over identified risks, ensuring that the PMO can proactively respond to emerging threats.

To begin with, establishing a robust risk monitoring framework is imperative. This framework should include well-defined procedures and tools for tracking risks throughout the project lifecycle. A risk register is an essential tool in this context. It serves as a centralized repository where all identified risks are documented, along with their respective statuses, mitigation strategies, and responsible parties. The risk register should be regularly updated to reflect the current state of each risk, providing a real-time overview of the risk landscape.

Quantitative and qualitative risk analysis techniques are fundamental in assessing the potential impact and likelihood of risks. Quantitative methods, such as Monte Carlo simulations and decision tree analysis, provide numerical estimations of risk impacts, facilitating data-driven decision-making. Qualitative techniques, such as risk probability and impact assessment matrices, enable the prioritization of risks based on their potential severity and likelihood of occurrence. These analyses help in determining which risks require immediate attention and which can be monitored for future developments.

Regular risk review meetings are essential for maintaining an up-to-date understanding of the risk environment. These meetings should involve key stakeholders, including project managers, risk owners, and senior management. During these sessions, participants review the current risk register, discuss newly identified risks, and evaluate the effectiveness of implemented mitigation strategies. Such collaborative discussions ensure that all relevant parties are aware of the risk status and can contribute to the development of comprehensive risk response plans.

Another critical aspect of monitoring risks is the use of Key Risk Indicators (KRIs). KRIs are metrics that provide early warning signals of potential risk events. By tracking these indicators, the PMO can detect signs of risk materialization before they fully impact the project. For instance, a KRI for a software development project might be the number of unresolved critical bugs. A rising trend in this metric could indicate a heightened risk of project delays, prompting preemptive action.

Technological tools and software play a significant role in enhancing risk monitoring capabilities. Advanced project management software often includes built-in risk management modules that facilitate real-time tracking and analysis of risks. These tools can automate the updating of the risk register, generate risk reports, and provide visual dashboards that highlight critical risk information. Leveraging such technology ensures that the PMO can efficiently manage and monitor risks, reducing the administrative burden on project teams.

Effective communication is paramount in the risk monitoring process. Transparent and timely communication channels must be established to ensure that all stakeholders are promptly informed of any significant risk developments. Regular risk reports, dashboards, and updates should be disseminated to keep everyone aligned. Additionally, fostering a culture of openness where team members feel comfortable reporting new risks or concerns is crucial for early risk identification and response.

Incorporating these strategies into the PMO's risk monitoring process ensures a proactive approach to risk management. By continuously tracking and assessing risks, the PMO can mitigate potential adverse impacts, maintain project stability, and enhance the likelihood of successful project outcomes.

Crisis Management

Effective crisis management is a critical component of a well-functioning Project Management Office (PMO). The ability to anticipate, identify, and mitigate crises can significantly influence the success of projects and the overall stability of the organization. A PMO must develop robust frameworks and strategies that enable swift and decisive action when unforeseen challenges arise.

The first step in crisis management involves establishing a comprehensive risk management plan. This plan should outline potential risks, their likelihood, and their potential impact on projects. By conducting a thorough risk assessment, the PMO can prioritize risks and allocate resources to mitigate the most significant threats. Regular updates to the risk management plan are essential, as new risks can emerge over time.

Effective communication is paramount during a crisis. The PMO should implement a clear communication strategy that ensures timely and accurate information dissemination to all stakeholders. This includes establishing predefined communication channels and protocols. Regular briefings and updates can help maintain transparency and build trust among team members, stakeholders, and clients. It is crucial to avoid misinformation and ensure that all parties are on the same page regarding the current status and next steps.

A well-defined escalation process is another vital element of crisis management. The PMO should identify key decision-makers and establish a hierarchy for escalating issues. This ensures that critical decisions are made swiftly and by the appropriate personnel. The escalation process should be well-documented and communicated to all team members to avoid confusion during high-pressure situations.

Another key aspect of crisis management is the development of contingency plans. These plans should provide alternative strategies and actions that can be implemented if primary plans fail. Contingency plans should be specific, actionable, and regularly tested through simulations or drills. By preparing for various scenarios, the PMO can respond more effectively when a crisis occurs.

Training and preparedness are also essential components of crisis management. The PMO should conduct regular training sessions for team members on crisis response procedures and protocols. This includes familiarizing them with the risk management plan, communication strategies, escalation processes, and contingency plans. Training should be ongoing to ensure that all team members are well-prepared to handle crises effectively.

Leveraging technology can enhance the PMO's crisis management capabilities. Tools such as project management software, communication platforms, and data analytics can provide real-time insights and facilitate rapid decision-making. The PMO should invest in technology that supports crisis management efforts and ensures that team members are proficient in using these tools.

Post-crisis evaluation is a critical step in improving crisis management practices. After a crisis has been resolved, the PMO should conduct a thorough review to identify what worked well and what areas need improvement. This evaluation should involve feedback from all stakeholders and result in actionable recommendations for future crises. By learning from past experiences, the PMO can continuously refine its crisis management strategies and enhance its overall resilience.

In conclusion, effective crisis management within a PMO requires a proactive approach that includes comprehensive risk assessment, clear communication, well-defined escalation processes, contingency planning, regular training, and the use of technology. By implementing these strategies, the PMO can navigate crises more effectively and ensure the continued success of its projects and the organization as a whole.

Chapter 13: PMO Best Practices

Industry Standards

The establishment of a Project Management Office (PMO) necessitates adherence to established industry standards to ensure efficacy and alignment with best practices. These standards provide a framework for consistent project delivery, risk management, and resource optimization. Recognizing the importance of industry standards, organizations can leverage them to streamline processes, enhance communication, and achieve strategic objectives.

The Project Management Institute (PMI) is a pivotal entity in the field of project management, offering widely recognized standards and certifications. The PMI's Project Management Body of Knowledge (PMBOK) Guide serves as a foundational reference, encompassing a comprehensive set of guidelines and best practices. The PMBOK Guide delineates five process groups: Initiating, Planning, Executing, Monitoring and Controlling, and Closing. Each group is integral to the project lifecycle, ensuring that projects are methodically planned and executed.

Adherence to PMBOK standards facilitates the establishment of a PMO that is both robust and adaptive. By integrating standardized processes, a PMO can ensure that project managers follow a uniform approach, reducing the likelihood of discrepancies and enhancing project predictability. Furthermore, PMBOK emphasizes the importance of tailoring processes to fit the specific context of an organization, allowing for flexibility while maintaining core principles.

The International Organization for Standardization (ISO) also provides critical standards relevant to PMOs. ISO 21500, Guidance on Project Management, offers high-level descriptions of concepts and processes that are considered to constitute good practice in project management. This standard aligns closely with PMBOK but focuses more on providing a general framework applicable across various industries. Implementing ISO 21500 can aid in the development of a PMO by ensuring that project management practices are coherent and universally applicable.

In addition to PMI and ISO standards, the Office of Government Commerce (OGC) in the United Kingdom has developed PRINCE2 (Projects IN Controlled Environments), a process-based method for effective project management. PRINCE2 is characterized by its emphasis on dividing projects into manageable and controllable stages. This method allows for greater control over resources and regular progress monitoring, which is particularly beneficial for PMOs seeking to maintain rigorous oversight of multiple projects simultaneously.

The Capability Maturity Model Integration (CMMI) framework is another critical standard that can enhance the effectiveness of a PMO. CMMI provides a structured view of process improvement across a project, program, and portfolio management. By progressing through CMMI's maturity levels, organizations can develop a PMO that is capable of continuous improvement, thereby increasing efficiency and effectiveness over time.

Moreover, the adoption of Agile methodologies has become increasingly prevalent in recent years. Agile frameworks such as Scrum, Kanban, and SAFe (Scaled Agile Framework) offer iterative and incremental approaches to project management. These methodologies prioritize flexibility, customer collaboration, and rapid delivery of value, which can complement traditional PMO structures. Integrating Agile practices within a PMO can enhance responsiveness to changes and foster a culture of continuous improvement.

Adopting these industry standards is not merely about compliance but about leveraging proven methodologies to enhance the strategic value of a PMO. By aligning with established standards, organizations can create a PMO that not only supports project success but also drives organizational growth and innovation. These standards serve as a benchmark for quality and effectiveness, enabling a PMO to function as a pivotal entity within the organizational structure.

Lessons Learned

A thorough examination of the establishment and operation of a Project Management Office (PMO) reveals several critical insights. These insights are pivotal for organizations aiming to create a PMO that significantly enhances project efficiency and aligns with strategic objectives.

Firstly, the importance of executive sponsorship cannot be overstated. A PMO requires strong support from senior management to ensure adequate resources, visibility, and authority. Without this backing, the PMO may struggle to implement standardized processes or enforce compliance, undermining its effectiveness. Engaging executives early in the process and maintaining their support through regular updates and demonstrated value is crucial.

Secondly, the PMO must be tailored to the specific needs of the organization. There is no one-size-fits-all approach, and the PMO's structure, processes, and tools should reflect the unique context of the organization. This customization involves understanding the organization's strategic goals, project portfolio, and existing project management maturity. Conducting a thorough needs assessment at the outset can guide the development of a PMO that addresses the organization's specific challenges and opportunities.

Another key lesson is the necessity of clear and consistent communication. Transparency in the PMO's objectives, processes, and benefits fosters buy-in from stakeholders across the organization. Regular communication channels, such as newsletters, meetings, and reports, help keep all parties informed and engaged. This transparency also aids in managing expectations and mitigating resistance to change.

The adaptability of the PMO is another critical factor. The business environment is dynamic, and the PMO must be able to evolve in response to changing organizational needs, market conditions, and technological advancements. Establishing a culture of continuous improvement within the PMO can facilitate this adaptability. Regular reviews and feedback loops enable the PMO to refine its processes and tools, ensuring sustained relevance and effectiveness.

Furthermore, the PMO should focus on delivering measurable value. Defining and tracking key performance indicators (KPIs) allows the organization to assess the PMO's impact on project success rates, resource utilization, and alignment with strategic goals. These metrics provide evidence of the PMO's contributions and can be instrumental in securing ongoing support from stakeholders.

An effective PMO also requires skilled personnel. Investing in the professional development of PMO staff ensures they possess the necessary competencies in project management methodologies, tools, and leadership. Providing opportunities for continuous learning and certification can enhance the PMO's capability to manage complex projects and drive organizational success.

Additionally, fostering a culture of collaboration is essential. The PMO should facilitate cooperation among project teams, departments, and stakeholders. This collaborative approach breaks down silos, promotes knowledge sharing, and leverages diverse perspectives to solve problems and innovate. Techniques such as cross-functional teams, workshops, and collaborative platforms can support this culture.

Lastly, the integration of technology is indispensable in modern PMO operations. Leveraging project management software, data analytics, and automation tools can increase efficiency, improve decision-making, and provide real-time insights into project performance. The selection of appropriate technological solutions should align with the PMO's objectives and the broader IT strategy of the organization.

These lessons underscore the multifaceted nature of establishing a successful PMO. By securing executive sponsorship, customizing the PMO to organizational needs, maintaining clear communication, being adaptable, delivering measurable value, investing in personnel, fostering collaboration, and integrating technology, organizations can create a PMO that drives project excellence and strategic alignment.

Continuous Improvement

The establishment of a Project Management Office (PMO) represents a significant milestone in the strategic alignment of project initiatives within an organization. However, the efficacy of a PMO is not static; it necessitates continuous refinement to adapt to evolving business needs and project complexities. Continuous improvement within a PMO framework is an iterative process grounded in the principles of feedback loops, performance metrics, and adaptive learning.

Central to continuous improvement is the systematic collection and analysis of performance data. Key Performance Indicators (KPIs) serve as quantifiable measures that provide insights into the efficiency, effectiveness, and overall health of the PMO. Common KPIs include project delivery times, budget adherence, resource utilization, and stakeholder satisfaction. By regularly monitoring these indicators, the PMO can identify areas requiring attention and implement targeted interventions.

The implementation of a robust feedback mechanism is paramount. Feedback should be solicited from a diverse range of stakeholders, including project managers, team members, and clients. This multidimensional input facilitates a comprehensive understanding of the PMO's performance from various perspectives. Structured feedback sessions, surveys, and retrospective meetings are effective methods for gathering actionable insights. The feedback should be meticulously analyzed to discern patterns and underlying issues that may not be immediately apparent.

One effective strategy for continuous improvement is the adoption of Agile methodologies. Agile principles emphasize flexibility, iterative progress, and responsiveness to change. By integrating Agile practices, the PMO can enhance its adaptability, ensuring that project management processes remain relevant and efficient. Techniques such as Scrum, Kanban, and Lean can be tailored to suit the specific needs of the PMO, fostering a culture of continuous learning and improvement.

Process standardization and documentation are critical components of a sustainable PMO. Standard Operating Procedures (SOPs) and best practice guidelines should be regularly reviewed and updated to reflect the latest insights and improvements. This ensures that all team members have access to current information, thereby reducing variability and enhancing consistency in project execution. Furthermore, documenting lessons learned from past projects is invaluable. These records serve as a knowledge repository that can inform future projects, preventing the recurrence of past mistakes and promoting best practices.

Training and professional development are essential for maintaining a high-performing PMO. Continuous improvement necessitates that project management personnel are well-versed in the latest tools, techniques, and methodologies. Regular training sessions, workshops, and certifications can significantly enhance the skill set of the PMO team, enabling them to tackle complex project challenges more effectively. Additionally, fostering a culture of knowledge sharing and collaboration within the PMO can lead to innovative solutions and improved performance.

Technological advancements offer significant opportunities for enhancing PMO operations. Project management software and tools that provide real-time data analytics, automation, and collaboration capabilities can streamline processes and improve decision-making. Investing in technology that aligns with the PMO's strategic goals can yield substantial improvements in efficiency and effectiveness.

Continuous improvement is an ongoing commitment that requires a proactive approach and a willingness to adapt. By systematically analyzing performance data, incorporating stakeholder feedback, adopting Agile methodologies, standardizing processes, investing in training, and leveraging technology, a PMO can achieve sustained excellence. This iterative process not only enhances the PMO's ability to deliver successful projects but also ensures its alignment with the dynamic needs of the organization.

Benchmarking Against Peers

Benchmarking against peers is a critical process for establishing and maintaining an effective Project Management Office (PMO). This practice involves comparing the performance, processes, and methodologies of one's PMO with those of similar organizations. Such comparisons are instrumental in identifying best practices, uncovering areas for improvement, and ensuring that the PMO remains competitive and efficient.

The initial step in benchmarking involves selecting appropriate peer organizations. These peers should have comparable project scopes, industry contexts, and organizational sizes. Selecting relevant peers ensures that the benchmarking process yields meaningful insights. Data collection from these organizations can be achieved through various means such as industry reports, case studies, surveys, and direct collaboration. It is crucial to ensure the accuracy and reliability of the data collected to make valid comparisons.

Quantitative metrics are often used in benchmarking to provide objective comparisons. Key performance indicators (KPIs) such as project completion rates, budget adherence, and resource utilization are commonly analyzed. By comparing these metrics against those of peers, a PMO can gauge its relative performance. For instance, if a PMO consistently completes projects on time and within budget at a higher rate than its peers, it can be considered highly effective in these areas.

However, quantitative analysis alone does not provide a complete picture. Qualitative factors such as stakeholder satisfaction, team morale, and innovation in project management practices are also essential. These factors can be assessed through interviews, surveys, and focus groups. By understanding the qualitative aspects of peer PMOs, organizations can adopt innovative practices and improve their own PMO's culture and effectiveness.

Benchmarking is not a one-time activity but an ongoing process. Regular benchmarking allows a PMO to stay updated with industry trends and continuously improve. It is beneficial to establish a systematic approach to benchmarking, including a schedule for periodic reviews and updates. This approach ensures that the PMO remains aligned with evolving best practices and industry standards.

One of the significant advantages of benchmarking is the ability to identify best practices that can be adopted or adapted. For example, a peer organization might employ a novel risk management strategy that has proven highly effective. By studying and implementing similar strategies, a PMO can enhance its own risk management processes. Additionally, benchmarking can reveal gaps and areas where a PMO is underperforming relative to its peers. Addressing these gaps can lead to substantial improvements in efficiency and effectiveness.

Collaboration with peer organizations can also enhance the benchmarking process. Sharing insights and experiences can lead to mutual learning and development. Industry conferences, workshops, and professional networks provide platforms for such collaborations. Engaging with peers through these channels facilitates the exchange of knowledge and best practices, contributing to the overall improvement of the PMO.

It is essential to recognize that benchmarking should be tailored to the specific context of the organization. What works for one PMO might not be directly applicable to another due to differences in organizational culture, project types, and strategic objectives. Therefore, while benchmarking provides valuable insights, it is important to adapt practices in a manner that aligns with the unique needs and goals of the organization.

By systematically benchmarking against peers, a PMO can ensure that it is not only keeping pace with industry standards but also striving for continuous improvement. This process is vital for maintaining a high level of performance and achieving long-term success in project management.

Success Stories

Numerous organizations have demonstrated the profound impact of establishing an effective Project Management Office (PMO). By examining these success stories, we can gain valuable insights into the strategies and practices that have led to significant improvements in project outcomes and organizational performance.

One notable example is a global telecommunications company that faced escalating project costs and frequent delays. The company implemented a centralized PMO to standardize project management practices across its diverse portfolio. This PMO introduced a robust project governance framework, incorporating standardized templates, risk management protocols, and performance metrics. Within two years, the company reported a 20% reduction in project costs and a 30% improvement in on-time delivery. The PMO's role in fostering a culture of accountability and continuous improvement was pivotal in achieving these results.

Another success story comes from a leading healthcare provider that struggled with fragmented project execution and resource allocation. The organization established a PMO with a mandate to streamline project selection and prioritization processes. By adopting a strategic alignment model, the PMO ensured that projects were closely linked to the organization's overall goals. The PMO also developed a comprehensive resource management system, enabling better allocation and utilization of personnel and financial resources. As a result, the healthcare provider experienced enhanced project efficiency, with a 25% increase in project success rates and improved patient care outcomes.

In the financial sector, a major bank sought to enhance its competitive edge by accelerating its digital transformation initiatives. The bank's PMO played a crucial role in orchestrating these efforts by implementing agile project management methodologies. The PMO introduced iterative development cycles, cross-functional teams, and continuous feedback loops, which allowed for greater flexibility and responsiveness to market demands. The bank reported a 40% increase in the speed of project delivery and a significant boost in customer satisfaction, attributing these achievements to the PMO's agile framework and effective stakeholder engagement.

A manufacturing giant also provides a compelling example of PMO success. Faced with the challenge of managing multiple complex projects across different regions, the company established a PMO to enhance coordination and oversight. The PMO introduced a centralized project tracking system, enabling real-time visibility into project progress and potential bottlenecks. This transparency facilitated proactive decision-making and risk mitigation. The company reported a 15% reduction in project lead times and a 10% increase in overall project quality. The PMO's emphasis on standardized processes and data-driven insights was instrumental in driving these improvements.

In the public sector, a government agency aimed to improve the efficiency of its infrastructure projects. The agency's PMO implemented a rigorous project management framework that included comprehensive planning, stakeholder engagement, and performance monitoring. The PMO also focused on building project management competencies through training and certification programs. The agency achieved notable success, with a 35% reduction in project overruns and enhanced public satisfaction with infrastructure services. The PMO's role in fostering a culture of professionalism and accountability was key to these outcomes.

These success stories underscore the transformative potential of an effective PMO. By standardizing practices, aligning projects with strategic objectives, and fostering a culture of continuous improvement, PMOs can drive significant enhancements in project performance and organizational effectiveness. The lessons learned from these examples provide a roadmap for other organizations seeking to establish or refine their own PMOs for optimal impact.

Chapter 14: Case Studies and Real-World Examples

Successful PMO Implementations

Effective PMO (Project Management Office) implementations are critical to ensuring the alignment of project outcomes with organizational goals. A successful PMO provides a structured framework that enhances project efficiency, governance, and strategic alignment. This subchapter elucidates the fundamental aspects and methodologies contributing to the successful establishment and operation of a PMO.

One of the primary determinants of a successful PMO is its strategic alignment with the organization's goals and objectives. This alignment ensures that the PMO's activities support the broader organizational strategy, facilitating better decision-making and resource allocation. To achieve this, it is essential to involve senior leadership in the PMO's formation and to secure their ongoing support. This top-down endorsement not only legitimizes the PMO but also ensures that it has the authority and resources necessary to implement its mandates effectively.

Another critical factor is the establishment of clear roles and responsibilities within the PMO. Defining these roles helps to avoid overlap and confusion, ensuring that each team member understands their specific duties and how they contribute to the PMO's overall objectives. This clarity also aids in the efficient distribution of tasks, fostering a collaborative environment where team members can leverage their unique skills and expertise.

Standardization of processes and methodologies is also crucial for a successful PMO. By developing and enforcing standardized project management practices, a PMO can ensure consistency, reduce errors, and enhance the predictability of project outcomes. This standardization often involves the adoption of recognized project management frameworks and methodologies, such as PMBOK (Project Management Body of Knowledge) or PRINCE2 (Projects IN Controlled Environments). These frameworks provide a structured approach to project management, encompassing best practices and guidelines that can be tailored to the organization's specific needs.

Effective communication is another cornerstone of a successful PMO. This involves not only the dissemination of information to stakeholders but also the establishment of robust feedback mechanisms. Regular updates and transparent reporting foster trust and ensure that all stakeholders are informed of project progress, risks, and issues. Additionally, feedback mechanisms enable the PMO to continuously improve its processes and address any concerns promptly.

The utilization of appropriate tools and technologies is also vital. Project management software, for instance, can streamline various aspects of project management, from scheduling and resource allocation to risk management and reporting. These tools enhance the PMO's ability to manage multiple projects simultaneously, providing real-time data and analytics that support informed decision-making.

Capacity building through continuous training and development is another essential element. Providing ongoing training opportunities for PMO staff ensures that they remain current with the latest project management trends, tools, and techniques. This not only enhances their individual capabilities but also strengthens the overall competency of the PMO.

Lastly, the establishment of performance metrics and KPIs (Key Performance Indicators) is imperative for monitoring and evaluating the PMO's effectiveness. These metrics should be aligned with the PMO's strategic objectives and provide quantifiable data on various aspects of project performance, such as on-time delivery, budget adherence, and stakeholder satisfaction. Regular performance reviews based on these metrics enable the PMO to identify areas for improvement and implement corrective actions as needed.

By focusing on these key areas—strategic alignment, clear roles and responsibilities, standardized processes, effective communication, appropriate tools and technologies, continuous training, and performance metrics—a PMO can significantly enhance its effectiveness and contribute to the successful delivery of projects.

Challenges Overcome

Implementing an effective Project Management Office (PMO) involves navigating a complex landscape of challenges that can impede progress. One of the primary obstacles is gaining executive buy-in. Securing support from top management is critical for the PMO's success, as it ensures the necessary resources and authority for the PMO to operate effectively. This requires a well-articulated business case that clearly demonstrates the value a PMO will bring to the organization, including improved project success rates, better resource management, and enhanced strategic alignment.

Another significant challenge is resistance to change. Organizational inertia can be a formidable barrier, as employees and managers may be accustomed to existing processes and skeptical of new methodologies. Overcoming this resistance necessitates a comprehensive change management strategy. This strategy should include clear communication of the benefits of the PMO, training programs to equip staff with new skills, and the involvement of key stakeholders in the PMO development process to foster a sense of ownership and acceptance.

Resource allocation is another critical hurdle. Establishing a PMO requires not just financial investment but also the allocation of skilled personnel. Organizations often struggle with reallocating their best project managers to the PMO, fearing it may detract from ongoing projects. To address this, it is essential to highlight the long-term benefits of having a centralized PMO, such as standardized processes and improved project outcomes, which ultimately benefit the entire organization.

Standardizing processes across various departments can also pose a challenge. Different departments may have developed their own project management practices, leading to a lack of uniformity and potential conflicts. To mitigate this, the PMO must develop and enforce standardized project management methodologies that are flexible enough to be adapted to specific departmental needs while maintaining overall consistency. This can be achieved through the creation of a central repository of project management templates and best practices, coupled with regular training sessions.

Another obstacle is maintaining continuous improvement. The initial setup of a PMO is only the beginning; it must evolve and adapt to changing organizational needs and project environments. This requires a feedback mechanism to capture lessons learned from completed projects and incorporate them into the PMO's processes. Regular audits and performance reviews can help identify areas for improvement and ensure that the PMO remains aligned with the organization's strategic goals.

Technology integration is also a significant challenge. The PMO must select and implement project management tools that facilitate collaboration, tracking, and reporting. The chosen tools must be compatible with existing systems and scalable to accommodate future needs. A phased implementation approach, starting with pilot projects, can help in identifying potential issues early and making necessary adjustments before a full-scale rollout.

Lastly, measuring the success of the PMO can be challenging. It is crucial to establish clear, quantifiable metrics that align with the organization's strategic objectives. These metrics should include project success rates, resource utilization, and stakeholder satisfaction. Regular reporting and analysis of these metrics will provide insights into the PMO's performance and areas needing improvement.

Through careful planning, effective communication, and a commitment to continuous improvement, these challenges can be successfully addressed, paving the way for a PMO that significantly enhances project delivery and organizational performance.

Innovative Solutions

Developing an effective Project Management Office (PMO) necessitates the integration of innovative solutions to address the dynamic challenges of contemporary project management. The inception of a robust PMO requires a comprehensive approach that leverages advanced technologies, methodologies, and frameworks to enhance efficiency, accountability, and strategic alignment.

A pivotal aspect of modern PMO innovation lies in the adoption of digital tools and platforms. Cloud-based project management software enables real-time collaboration, data sharing, and communication across geographically dispersed teams. Such tools facilitate seamless integration with existing enterprise systems, ensuring that project data is consistently updated and accessible. Automation of routine tasks, such as scheduling, reporting, and resource allocation, reduces manual errors and frees up valuable time for project managers to focus on strategic decision-making.

Artificial Intelligence (AI) and Machine Learning (ML) are transformative technologies that can significantly enhance PMO capabilities. Predictive analytics, driven by AI, provide insights into potential project risks and opportunities by analyzing historical data and identifying patterns. This predictive capability enables proactive risk management and informed decision-making. ML algorithms can optimize resource allocation by predicting workforce availability and skill requirements, thereby ensuring that the right resources are deployed at the right time.

Agile methodologies have gained prominence as a means to foster flexibility and responsiveness within the PMO framework. Agile practices, such as iterative development, continuous feedback, and cross-functional collaboration, enable project teams to adapt to changing requirements and deliver incremental value. Implementing Agile methodologies within a PMO requires a cultural shift towards embracing change and encouraging innovation at all organizational levels. Hybrid models that combine Agile with traditional project management approaches can be particularly effective in balancing structure with flexibility.

The integration of data analytics is another critical innovation for PMOs. Advanced data analytics tools allow for the collection, processing, and visualization of project data, providing actionable insights into project performance and trends. Key performance indicators (KPIs) and metrics can be tracked in real-time, enabling project managers to make data-driven decisions and adjust strategies promptly. Dashboards and reporting tools offer a centralized view of project health, facilitating transparency and accountability.

Blockchain technology presents a novel solution for enhancing transparency and security within the PMO. By creating immutable records of project transactions and milestones, blockchain ensures data integrity and reduces the risk of fraud. Smart contracts, which are self-executing contracts with the terms directly written into code, can automate and enforce project agreements, reducing administrative overhead and ensuring compliance.

Fostering a culture of continuous improvement is essential for sustaining innovation within a PMO. Regular training and development programs for project managers and team members ensure that they remain abreast of the latest tools, techniques, and best practices. Encouraging knowledge sharing and collaboration across projects promotes the dissemination of innovative ideas and solutions. Establishing a feedback loop where lessons learned from completed projects are systematically analyzed and integrated into future projects enhances organizational learning and project outcomes.

The implementation of innovative solutions within a PMO is not without challenges. Resistance to change, initial costs, and the need for upskilling the workforce are common hurdles. However, the long-term benefits of increased efficiency, improved project outcomes, and strategic alignment far outweigh these initial obstacles. A strategic approach to innovation, underpinned by a commitment to continuous improvement, positions the PMO as a pivotal driver of organizational success in an increasingly complex and competitive landscape.

Lessons Learned

Throughout the process of establishing an effective Project Management Office (PMO), several critical insights have been garnered. These insights not only illuminate the path to successful PMO implementation but also underscore common pitfalls and best practices that can significantly enhance the efficacy of a PMO.

One of the foremost lessons is the paramount importance of executive sponsorship and support. A PMO cannot thrive in isolation; it requires the backing of senior leadership to secure necessary resources, overcome resistance, and align the PMO's objectives with the strategic goals of the organization. Without this high-level endorsement, the PMO risks being marginalized and underfunded, which can severely undermine its potential impact.

Another key insight pertains to the necessity of a clear and well-communicated vision. The PMO must have a defined mission statement that articulates its purpose, value proposition, and the benefits it aims to deliver. This vision should be communicated effectively across all levels of the organization to ensure buy-in and to foster a culture of collaboration. Ambiguity in the PMO's objectives can lead to misaligned expectations and diminished effectiveness.

The selection of the PMO leadership team is crucial. Leaders should possess not only technical project management skills but also strong interpersonal and change management capabilities. Effective PMO leaders act as change agents who can inspire and guide project managers and stakeholders through the complexities of project execution. Their ability to navigate organizational politics and foster an environment of trust and transparency is indispensable.

Standardization and flexibility must be balanced. While the establishment of standardized processes and methodologies is essential for consistency and efficiency, the PMO must also remain adaptable to the specific needs and contexts of different projects. Rigid adherence to a one-size-fits-all approach can stifle innovation and responsiveness, whereas a flexible framework allows for customization without sacrificing the benefits of standardization.

The integration of robust metrics and performance indicators is another critical lesson. The PMO must implement a comprehensive set of KPIs that measure not only project outcomes but also process efficiency and stakeholder satisfaction. These metrics should be reviewed regularly to identify areas for improvement and to demonstrate the PMO's value to the organization. Data-driven decision making enhances the PMO's ability to deliver successful projects consistently.

Effective communication cannot be overstated. The PMO must establish clear channels for communication both within the project teams and with external stakeholders. Regular status updates, transparent reporting, and open forums for feedback are essential components of a communication strategy that builds trust and keeps all parties informed and engaged.

The importance of continuous improvement is another salient lesson. The PMO should adopt a mindset of ongoing learning and refinement. This involves not only the regular review of processes and outcomes but also staying abreast of industry best practices and emerging trends in project management. By fostering a culture of continuous improvement, the PMO can remain dynamic and responsive to the evolving needs of the organization.

Lastly, stakeholder engagement and management are critical to the PMO's success. Engaging stakeholders early and often ensures that their needs and concerns are addressed, thereby enhancing their support and collaboration. Effective stakeholder management strategies include regular consultations, transparent communication, and the incorporation of stakeholder feedback into the PMO's practices and processes.

These lessons provide a foundational framework for creating an effective PMO that delivers tangible value to the organization. By adhering to these principles, organizations can establish a PMO that not only manages projects efficiently but also drives strategic objectives and fosters a culture of continuous improvement.

Future Trends

The landscape of Project Management Offices (PMOs) is undergoing significant transformation, driven by technological advancements, evolving business needs, and the increasing complexity of project environments. As organizations strive to enhance their project management capabilities, several future trends are anticipated to shape the development and operation of effective PMOs.

One prominent trend is the integration of artificial intelligence (AI) and machine learning (ML) into PMO processes. These technologies offer the potential to revolutionize project management by automating routine tasks, enhancing decision-making, and providing predictive analytics. AI can assist in risk management by identifying potential issues before they escalate, while ML algorithms can analyze historical data to forecast project outcomes more accurately. The adoption of AI and ML is expected to streamline project workflows, reduce human error, and improve overall project efficiency.

Another significant trend is the increasing importance of data analytics in PMO operations. The ability to harness and analyze large volumes of project data enables PMOs to gain deeper insights into project performance and resource utilization. Advanced analytics tools can help PMOs identify patterns, trends, and anomalies, facilitating more informed decision-making. By leveraging data-driven insights, PMOs can optimize project schedules, allocate resources more effectively, and anticipate potential bottlenecks. The shift towards data-centric PMOs underscores the critical role of data in driving project success.

The rise of remote and hybrid work models is also influencing the future of PMOs. The COVID-19 pandemic has accelerated the adoption of remote work, prompting PMOs to adapt to new ways of managing distributed teams. Virtual collaboration tools, cloud-based project management software, and digital communication platforms are becoming essential components of the modern PMO toolkit. These technologies enable PMOs to maintain project visibility, ensure seamless communication, and foster collaboration among team members, regardless of their physical location. The ability to effectively manage remote and hybrid teams will be a key competency for future PMOs.

Agile methodologies continue to gain traction in the project management domain, and their influence on PMOs is expected to grow. Agile practices emphasize flexibility, iterative development, and continuous improvement, making them well-suited for dynamic project environments. PMOs are increasingly adopting agile frameworks to enhance their responsiveness to changing project requirements and stakeholder needs. The integration of agile methodologies within PMOs promotes a culture of adaptability and innovation, enabling organizations to deliver value more rapidly and efficiently.

Sustainability and social responsibility are emerging as critical considerations for PMOs. As organizations become more conscious of their environmental and social impact, PMOs are being tasked with incorporating sustainability principles into project planning and execution. This involves adopting green project management practices, such as minimizing resource consumption, reducing waste, and promoting eco-friendly solutions. Additionally, PMOs are expected to align projects with broader corporate social responsibility (CSR) goals, ensuring that project outcomes contribute positively to society and the environment. The emphasis on sustainability reflects a growing recognition of the interconnectedness between business success and societal well-being.

The future of PMOs is also characterized by a greater focus on talent development and capability building. As the project management landscape evolves, there is a heightened demand for skilled project managers who can navigate complex project environments and leverage emerging technologies. PMOs are investing in continuous learning and professional development programs to equip their teams with the necessary skills and knowledge. This includes training in advanced project management techniques, technology proficiency, and leadership development. By fostering a culture of continuous improvement, PMOs can ensure that their teams remain agile and capable of addressing future challenges.

In conclusion, the future trends shaping PMOs are driven by technological innovation, data analytics, evolving work models, agile methodologies, sustainability, and talent development. These trends present both opportunities and challenges for PMOs as they strive to enhance their effectiveness and deliver value in an increasingly complex project landscape. Organizations that proactively adapt to these trends will be well-positioned to create and sustain effective PMOs that drive project success.

Chapter 15: Future of PMO

Emerging Trends

The landscape of project management is continuously evolving, driven by technological advancements, organizational needs, and market dynamics. One of the most significant emerging trends in project management offices (PMOs) is the integration of advanced analytics and artificial intelligence (AI). These technologies are transforming how PMOs function, enabling more accurate forecasting, resource allocation, and risk management. Advanced analytics allow PMOs to harness big data, providing insights that were previously unattainable. AI, on the other hand, automates routine tasks, freeing up project managers to focus on strategic decision-making.

Another critical trend is the shift towards agile methodologies. Traditional PMOs often relied on waterfall models, which, while structured, lacked flexibility. Agile methodologies promote iterative progress, adaptability, and stakeholder collaboration, making them particularly suitable for today's fast-paced business environment. This shift is not merely a change in process but a fundamental transformation in how projects are conceptualized and executed. PMOs are now required to foster a culture of continuous improvement and responsiveness, aligning closely with agile principles.

Furthermore, the rise of remote work has necessitated the adoption of digital collaboration tools. With teams dispersed across various geographies, PMOs must leverage platforms that facilitate seamless communication and coordination. Tools such as Slack, Microsoft Teams, and Asana have become indispensable, ensuring that project timelines are met and that team members remain aligned despite physical distances. This trend underscores the importance of digital literacy within PMOs and the need for robust cybersecurity measures to protect sensitive project data.

The growing emphasis on sustainability and corporate social responsibility (CSR) is also influencing PMO practices. Organizations are increasingly held accountable for their environmental and social impacts, compelling PMOs to incorporate sustainability metrics into their project evaluation criteria. This trend is driving the development of green project management practices, which prioritize resource efficiency, waste reduction, and ethical considerations. PMOs are now tasked with balancing traditional project success metrics—such as time, cost, and scope—with these emerging sustainability goals.

Additionally, the concept of hybrid PMOs is gaining traction. Hybrid PMOs blend traditional and agile methodologies, offering a flexible approach that can be tailored to the specific needs of a project. This model allows PMOs to leverage the strengths of both frameworks, ensuring that projects are managed efficiently while remaining adaptable to change. The implementation of hybrid PMOs requires a deep understanding of both methodologies and the ability to seamlessly integrate them within the organizational context.

The role of the PMO is also expanding beyond project execution to encompass strategic alignment and value delivery. Modern PMOs are expected to act as strategic partners, aligning projects with organizational goals and driving business value. This expanded role necessitates a broader skill set, including strategic planning, stakeholder management, and change management. PMOs are increasingly involved in portfolio management, ensuring that the right projects are prioritized and that resources are optimally allocated to maximize returns.

In conclusion, the evolution of PMOs is characterized by the integration of advanced technologies, the adoption of agile and hybrid methodologies, the emphasis on digital collaboration, the focus on sustainability, and the expanded strategic role. These trends are reshaping how PMOs operate, driving greater efficiency, adaptability, and alignment with organizational objectives. As these trends continue to develop, PMOs must remain agile and forward-thinking, continuously adapting to the changing landscape of project management.

Impact of Technology

The integration of technology within a Project Management Office (PMO) is a critical factor that can significantly influence its effectiveness and efficiency. Modern technological advancements equip PMOs with tools that enhance project management processes, streamline communication, and improve data accuracy. This subchapter explores the multifaceted impact of technology on the establishment and operation of an effective PMO.

Project management software is central to the technological framework of a PMO. These platforms offer functionalities such as task scheduling, resource allocation, and progress tracking. Advanced software solutions provide real-time data analytics and reporting capabilities, enabling project managers to make informed decisions promptly. The automation of routine tasks reduces the likelihood of human error and frees up valuable time for project managers to focus on strategic planning and problem-solving.

Cloud computing has revolutionized the way PMOs handle data storage and accessibility. Cloud-based solutions ensure that project data is accessible from anywhere, facilitating remote work and collaboration among geographically dispersed teams. This accessibility is crucial in today's globalized work environment, where team members may be spread across different time zones. Moreover, cloud computing offers scalable storage solutions, allowing PMOs to manage large volumes of data without the need for substantial investments in physical infrastructure.

The advent of artificial intelligence (AI) and machine learning (ML) technologies introduces new dimensions to project management. AI-driven tools can predict project risks, optimize resource allocation, and provide insights based on historical data. Machine learning algorithms can analyze patterns and trends, offering predictive analytics that help in forecasting project timelines and potential bottlenecks. These technologies empower PMOs to adopt a proactive approach, mitigating risks before they escalate into significant issues.

Communication technologies play a pivotal role in enhancing collaboration within a PMO. Tools such as instant messaging, video conferencing, and collaborative workspaces ensure seamless communication among team members. Effective communication is vital for the successful execution of projects, as it ensures that all stakeholders are aligned and informed about project progress and changes. These tools also support the integration of feedback mechanisms, allowing for continuous improvement and adaptation throughout the project lifecycle.

Data security is an essential consideration in the technological landscape of a PMO. With the increasing reliance on digital tools and cloud-based platforms, safeguarding sensitive project data becomes paramount. Implementing robust cybersecurity measures, such as encryption, multi-factor authentication, and regular security audits, is necessary to protect against data breaches and cyber threats. Ensuring data integrity and confidentiality fosters trust among stakeholders and preserves the credibility of the PMO.

The use of technology in a PMO also extends to stakeholder management. Customer relationship management (CRM) systems and stakeholder engagement tools help in tracking interactions, managing expectations, and maintaining transparent communication channels with clients and stakeholders. These systems contribute to building strong relationships and ensuring that stakeholder needs and concerns are addressed promptly and effectively.

Technology's impact on PMO effectiveness is profound and multifaceted. The strategic implementation of project management software, cloud computing, AI, communication tools, and data security measures can transform the way PMOs operate. By leveraging these technological advancements, PMOs can enhance their capabilities, drive project success, and deliver value to their organizations. As technology continues to evolve, PMOs must remain adaptable and forward-thinking, continuously exploring new tools and methodologies to stay ahead in the competitive landscape of project management.

Evolving Roles and Responsibilities

The establishment and development of a Project Management Office (PMO) necessitate a clear understanding of roles and responsibilities, which are subject to evolution as the PMO matures. Initially, the PMO's primary function is often focused on the standardization of project management practices and methodologies. Over time, however, the scope of the PMO's responsibilities expands to encompass strategic alignment, governance, and continuous improvement processes.

In the nascent stages of a PMO, roles are typically centered around the foundational elements of project management. Key responsibilities include the implementation of consistent project management processes, development of templates and tools, and provision of training and support for project managers. At this stage, the PMO acts as a repository of best practices and a source of guidance for project execution.

As the PMO progresses, its role evolves to include the integration of project management processes with organizational strategy. This involves aligning project selection and prioritization with strategic objectives, ensuring that projects contribute to the broader goals of the organization. The PMO begins to play a critical role in portfolio management, overseeing the selection, initiation, and monitoring of projects to ensure optimal resource utilization and value delivery.

Governance is another critical area that evolves within the PMO's purview. Initially, governance may be focused on compliance with project management standards and methodologies. However, as the PMO matures, governance expands to encompass broader oversight of project performance, risk management, and stakeholder engagement. The PMO establishes frameworks for project audits, performance reviews, and risk assessments, ensuring that projects adhere to organizational standards and deliver expected outcomes.

The continuous improvement of project management practices is also a key responsibility that evolves over time. In the early stages, the PMO may focus on basic process improvements and the adoption of industry best practices. As the PMO matures, continuous improvement efforts become more sophisticated, involving the analysis of project performance data, identification of process inefficiencies, and implementation of corrective actions. The PMO fosters a culture of learning and adaptation, encouraging project teams to share lessons learned and implement improvements on an ongoing basis.

The roles within the PMO also evolve in response to the changing needs of the organization. Initially, the PMO may be staffed with project management professionals who focus on the execution of specific tasks. As the PMO's responsibilities expand, roles may diversify to include portfolio managers, governance specialists, and continuous improvement experts. This diversification of roles ensures that the PMO can effectively manage its expanded scope of responsibilities and deliver value across the organization.

Effective communication and stakeholder engagement are critical throughout the evolution of the PMO's roles and responsibilities. The PMO must establish clear lines of communication with project teams, senior management, and other stakeholders to ensure alignment and support for its initiatives. Regular reporting, stakeholder meetings, and feedback mechanisms are essential for maintaining transparency and fostering collaboration.

In summary, the evolving roles and responsibilities of a PMO reflect its transition from a focus on project management standardization to a strategic, governance, and continuous improvement function. This evolution requires a dynamic approach to role definition, an ongoing commitment to aligning with organizational objectives, and a proactive stance on governance and continuous improvement. By adapting to the changing needs of the organization, the PMO can effectively support project success and drive value creation.

Globalization and PMO

In recent decades, the phenomenon of globalization has significantly influenced the structure and operations of Project Management Offices (PMOs). The interconnectedness of markets, technologies, and cultures necessitates a comprehensive understanding of how global dynamics impact project management practices. This subchapter examines the critical aspects of globalization that affect PMOs and offers insights into adapting strategies to ensure efficiency and effectiveness in this global context.

One of the primary implications of globalization on PMOs is the diversification of project teams. With the increasing trend of cross-border collaborations, PMOs must manage teams composed of members from different cultural backgrounds.

This diversity offers various perspectives and innovative solutions but also presents challenges in terms of communication, coordination, and conflict resolution. Effective PMOs implement cultural competency training and leverage communication tools that facilitate seamless interaction among team members, regardless of their geographic location.

Globalization also impacts the regulatory and compliance landscape for PMOs. Projects that span multiple countries must adhere to a complex web of local, national, and international regulations. This requires PMOs to stay abreast of legal and regulatory changes in different jurisdictions. An effective PMO will establish a robust compliance framework, ensuring all project activities align with relevant laws and standards. This framework often includes dedicated roles or teams focused on monitoring and enforcing compliance across all project phases.

The influence of globalization extends to resource management within PMOs. Access to a global talent pool allows PMOs to tap into specialized skills and expertise that may not be available locally. However, this also introduces challenges related to time zone differences, language barriers, and varying work practices. Effective resource management strategies, such as utilizing global resource management software and implementing flexible working arrangements, are essential in overcoming these challenges.

Technology plays a pivotal role in enabling PMOs to operate effectively in a globalized environment. Advanced project management tools and platforms facilitate real-time collaboration, data sharing, and project tracking across different regions. These technologies not only enhance efficiency but also provide valuable insights through data analytics, enabling PMOs to make informed decisions. Investing in state-of-the-art project management software and ensuring its adoption across the organization is a critical step for PMOs operating in a global context.

Risk management is another area where globalization exerts a significant impact. Global projects are exposed to a broader range of risks, including geopolitical instability, economic fluctuations, and cultural misunderstandings. PMOs must adopt a proactive approach to risk management, identifying potential risks early and developing mitigation strategies. This often involves conducting thorough risk assessments and establishing contingency plans that can be quickly implemented in response to unforeseen events.

The global nature of modern business also necessitates a strategic approach to stakeholder management. PMOs must navigate the interests and expectations of a diverse range of stakeholders, including international clients, partners, and regulatory bodies. Effective stakeholder management involves clear communication, regular updates, and fostering strong relationships with all parties involved. Understanding the cultural nuances and business practices of different stakeholders is crucial for maintaining positive and productive interactions.

In summary, globalization presents both opportunities and challenges for PMOs. By adopting strategies that address cultural diversity, regulatory compliance, resource management, technological integration, risk management, and stakeholder engagement, PMOs can enhance their effectiveness and adaptability in a globalized world. The ability to navigate these complexities is essential for PMOs to deliver successful projects that meet the demands of an increasingly interconnected and dynamic global market.

Sustainability and PMO

The integration of sustainability principles within a Project Management Office (PMO) has become increasingly pertinent in today's corporate environment. Sustainability, encompassing environmental, social, and economic dimensions, necessitates a comprehensive approach to project management that aligns with long-term organizational goals. The PMO, as a centralized entity for managing and standardizing project processes, plays a crucial role in embedding sustainability into the core of project management practices.

To effectively integrate sustainability, the PMO must first establish a clear framework that defines sustainability objectives and metrics. These objectives should align with the organization's overarching sustainability strategy and be incorporated into the PMO's governance structure. This involves developing policies and procedures that mandate the consideration of sustainability criteria at every stage of the project lifecycle, from initiation through to closure.

One of the primary mechanisms for embedding sustainability within the PMO is through the adoption of sustainable project management methodologies. These methodologies emphasize the integration of sustainability criteria into project planning, execution, and monitoring. For instance, the inclusion of environmental impact assessments as a standard component of project planning ensures that potential negative impacts are identified and mitigated early in the project lifecycle. Similarly, adopting lifecycle cost analysis can help in evaluating the long-term economic benefits of sustainable practices over short-term financial gains.

The PMO should also focus on capacity building and training to ensure that project managers and team members possess the necessary skills and knowledge to implement sustainable practices. This can be achieved through targeted training programs, workshops, and continuous professional development opportunities that emphasize the importance of sustainability in project management. Furthermore, the PMO can facilitate knowledge sharing and best practices by creating platforms for collaboration and communication among project teams.

Monitoring and reporting are critical components of integrating sustainability into the PMO. Establishing key performance indicators (KPIs) that measure sustainability outcomes allows the PMO to track progress and identify areas for improvement. These KPIs should be aligned with industry standards and benchmarks to ensure consistency and comparability. Regular reporting on sustainability performance not only promotes transparency and accountability but also provides valuable insights for continuous improvement.

Moreover, stakeholder engagement is essential for the successful integration of sustainability within the PMO. Engaging with stakeholders, including clients, suppliers, and community members, helps in understanding their expectations and incorporating their feedback into project planning and execution. This collaborative approach ensures that sustainability initiatives are not only feasible but also supported by those who are impacted by the projects.

Technology can also play a pivotal role in supporting sustainability efforts within the PMO. The use of project management software and tools that incorporate sustainability metrics can streamline the process of tracking and reporting sustainability performance. Additionally, leveraging data analytics and artificial intelligence can provide deeper insights into sustainability trends and help in making informed decisions.

The PMO should advocate for a culture of sustainability within the organization. This involves promoting sustainability as a core value and encouraging behaviors that support sustainable practices. Recognizing and rewarding project teams that achieve sustainability goals can further reinforce this culture and motivate continuous improvement.

Incorporating sustainability into the PMO is not without challenges. It requires a shift in mindset and a commitment to long-term thinking. However, the benefits of sustainable project management, including enhanced reputation, cost savings, and risk mitigation, make it a worthwhile endeavor. By systematically integrating sustainability into its processes and practices, the PMO can drive meaningful change and contribute to the overall sustainability goals of the organization.

www.ingramcontent.com/pod-product-compliance
Lightning Source LLC
Chambersburg PA
CBHW031615210526
45464CB00004B/1587